Edited by
LORNA WING

Aspects of Autism: Biological Research

Proceedings of a conference held at the University of Kent, 18–20 September, 1987.

Gaskell/The National Autistic Society

©The Royal College of Psychiatrists 1988

ISBN 0 902241 25 7

Gaskell is an imprint of the Royal College of Psychiatrists,
17 Belgrave Square, London SW1

Distributed in North America
by American Psychiatric Press, Inc.

Phototypeset by Dobbie Typesetting Limited, Plymouth, Devon
Printed in Great Britain at the Alden Press, Oxford

Contents

List of Contributors

Catherine Barthélémy, Lecturer in Developmental Neurophysiology and Child Psychiatry, Bretonneau Hospital, University of Tours, France

N. Buneau, Researcher, INSERM U316, Bretonneau Hospital, University of Tours, France

Ann Le Couteur, Lecturer, Institute of Psychiatry, and Honorary Consultant, The Maudsley Hospital, London

Uta Frith, Scientist, MRC Cognitive Development Unit, London

B. Garreau, Lecturer in Developmental Neurophysiology and Child Psychiatry, Bretonneau Hospital, University of Tours, France

Christopher Gillberg, Professor of Child and Youth Psychiatry, University of Göteborg, Sweden

J. Jouve, Researcher, Department of Biochemistry, Bretonneau Hospital, University of Tours, France

Janice Kohler, Senior Paediatric Registrar, Southampton General Hospital

G. Lelord, Professor of Physiology and Psychiatry, Bretonneau Hospital, University of Tours, France

J. Martineau, Researcher, INSERM U316, Bretonneau Hospital, University of Tours, France

S. Roux, Analyst, Bretonneau Hospital, University of Tours, France

Frederick J. Rowell, Principal Lecturer, Department of Pharmaceutical Chemistry, Sunderland Polytechnic

Paul Shattock, Senior Lecturer in Pharmacognosy, Department of Pharmaceutical Chemistry, Sunderland Polytechnic

E. Gene Stubbs, Associate Professor, Crippled Children's Division, Department of Psychiatry, School of Medicine, Oregon Health Sciences University, Portland, Oregon, USA

Lynn Waterhouse, Professor of Linguistics, Trenton State College, New Jersey

Lorna Wing, Scientific Staff, MRC Social Psychiatry Unit, Institute of Psychiatry, London

Preface   The autistic continuum

LORNA WING

Kanner first described the pattern of abnormal behaviour he called 'early infantile autism' in 1943. He emphasised that, in his opinion, severe impairment of the capacity to interact socially with other people was the most essential feature. Children showing all the items as listed by Kanner are comparatively rare (estimates vary around 2–4 per 10 000 children). However, there are many more who are severely impaired in social interaction, and who share other features with Kanner's autism, but in whom the manifestations are not precisely as Kanner described. Typical autism shades into these other conditions with no sharp borderline. The prevalence for all children with social impairment, including typical autism, is in the region of 15–20 per 10 000 (Wing & Gould, 1979).

The full range of these problems is referred to here as the 'autistic continuum' or spectrum and is more or less equivalent to the group of Pervasive Developmental Disorders as described in DSM–III–Revised (the latest version of the American Psychiatric Association's *Diagnostic and Statistical Manual*, 1987).

In Table I, the clinical features which may be found within the complete spectrum are enumerated and described. Some sets of criteria for defining 'typical' autism proposed by different authors or groups of workers are shown for comparison in Table II. The numbers in this table refer to those in Table I. Only those systems which specify essential criteria are included. Descriptions by authors or committees published without directions as to which features must be present — for example, the ninth edition of the *International Classification of Diseases* (World Health Organization, 1977) or the Nine Points of the committee chaired by Mildred Creak (1964) — are not mentioned. Systems depending upon adding up points from a rating scale are also excluded (e.g. Rimland, 1968, 1971).

It will be seen that, although the sets of criteria overlap, they are by no means identical. However, careful examination will show that all authors emphasise the social impairments, especially aloofness and indifference to others, at least in the early years.

TABLE I
The autistic continuum
(features most often used in diagnosis[1])

Item	*Manifestations*[2]			
	1 *Tend to be seen in the most severely handicapped/retarded*	2	3	4 *Tend to be seen in the least severely handicapped/retarded*
Social interaction	1 Aloof and indifferent	2 Approaches for physical needs only	3 Passively accepts approaches	4 Makes bizarre one-sided approaches
Social communication (verbal and non-verbal)	1 No communication	2 Needs only	3 Replies if approached	4 Spontaneous, but repetitive, one-sided, odd
Social imagination	1 No imagination	2 Copies others mechanically	3 Uses dolls, toys correctly but limited, uncreative, repetitive	4 Acts out one theme (e.g. Batman) repetitively; may use other children as 'mechanical aids'
Repetitive pattern of self-chosen activities	1 Simple, bodily-directed (e.g. face-tapping, self-injury)	2 Simple, object-directed (e.g. taps, spins, switches lights)	3 Complex routines, manipulation of objects, or movements (e.g. bedtime ritual, lining up objects, attachment to objects, whole-body movements)	4 Verbal, abstract (e.g. timetables, movements of planets, repetitive questioning)
Language — formal system	1 No language	2 Limited — mostly echolalic	3 Incorrect use of pronouns, prepositions; idiosyncratic use of words/phrases; odd constructions	4 Grammatical but long-winded, repetitive, literal interpretations
Responses to sensory stimuli (oversensitive to sound, fascinated by lights, touches, tastes, self-spinning; smells objects or people; indifferent to pain, heat, cold etc.)	1 Very marked	2 Marked	3 Occasional	4 Minimal or absent
Movements (flaps, jumps, rocks, tiptoe walking, odd hand postures etc.)	1 Very marked	2 Marked	3 Occasional	4 Minimal or absent
Special skills (manipulation of mechanical objects; music; drawing; mathematics; rote memory; constructional skills etc.)	1 No special skills	2 One skill better than others but all below chronological age	3 One skill around chronological age — rest well below	4 One skill at high level well above chronological age, very different from other abilities

1. There are other clinical features seen in disorders in the autistic continuum, but they are not listed here because they are not mentioned in the various sets of criteria considered *essential* for diagnosis.
2. The manifestations of each item (numbered 1 to 4 under each heading) are arbitrarily chosen points along a continuum. In reality, each shades into the next without any clear divisions.

TABLE II
Comparison of diagnostic criteria[1]
(The numbers refer to those in Table I; for ',' read 'or')

Abnormalities of:	Typical autism					Recent amendments to international criteria		Asperger's syndrome	Autistic continuum
	Kanner (1943)	Lotter (1966)	Rutter (1978)	ASA[5] (1988)	DSM-III (APA, 1980)	Draft ICD-10 (WHO, 1987)[2]	DSM-III-R (APA, 1987)	Wing (1981)	Wing & Gould (1979)
Social interaction	1,2	1,2	1,2	1,2	1,2	1,2,3,4[4]	1,2,3,4[1]	3,4	1,2,3,4
Social communication	1,2	1,2	1,2,3,4	1,2	1,2	1,2,3,4	1,2,3,4	3,4	1,2,3,4
Social imagination	—	—	1,3	—	—	1,2,3,4	1,2,3,4	4	1,2,3,4
Repetitive activities	3	3	3,4	2,3[3]	2,3[3]	2,3,4		4	1,2,3,4
Language	1,2,3	—	1,2,3	1,2,3[3]	1,2[3]	—	—	4	—
Sensory responses	—	—	—	1,2[3]	—	—	—	—	—
Movements	—	—	—	1,2[3]	—	—	—	—	—
Special skills	3	—	—	—	4[3]	—	—	4	—
Other	Attractive appearance; no organic aetiology	—	—	Disturbed sequence and rates of development	No delusions or hallucinations	Excludes other causes of clinical picture	Must be at least 8 examples of impairment in total, from among the 4 areas	Clumsy	—
Age of onset	0–2½	—	0–2½	—	0–2½	0–3	—	—	—

1. Most workers imply that the characteristic features have to be present in early life, but may become less obvious or change in manifestation in middle or later childhood. However, none has specified precisely the age up to which the features must be present to make a diagnosis, except Lotter, who specified up to 7 or 8 years, and Rutter, who specified up to around 5 years.
2. ICD–10, 1987, draft of chapter V, categories F00–F99. Mental, behavioural and developmental disorders: clinical descriptions and diagnostic guidelines. MNH/MEP/87.1 Rev. 1.
3. At least *one* example of *any one* of these types of impairment is sufficient.
4. At least *two* examples from each of these types of impairment must be present.
5. Autism Society of America.

The criteria used affect prevalence rates and may also influence other research findings. The often quoted figure of 4–5 per 10 000 refers to the numbers found using Lotter's (1966) criteria only. One of the effects of the differences in the criteria is to alter the IQ range of the children diagnosed as autistic. For example, Kanner's insistence on good manipulative or rote memory skills excludes many severely retarded children and virtually all those who are profoundly retarded. On the other hand, the Autism Society of America's (1988) definition, with its insistence on odd movements or odd responses to sensory stimuli, and lack of mention of special skills, shifts down to a lower IQ band, though overlapping with Kanner's group. The criteria for Asperger's syndrome used by Wing (1981) ensure that only people in the more able end of the continuum are included, whereas Wing & Gould's definition of the whole autistic continuum includes all intelligence levels from profound retardation to average and above.

References

AMERICAN PSYCHIATRIC ASSOCIATION (1980) *Diagnostic and Statistical Manual of Mental Disorders* (3rd edn) (DSM–III). Washington: APA.
—— (1987) *Diagnostic and Statistical Manual of Mental Disorders* (3rd edn, revised) (DSM–III–R). Washington: APA.
AUTISM SOCIETY OF AMERICA (1988) *The Advocate*, **20**, 24.
CREAK, M. (1964) Schizophrenic syndrome in childhood: further progress report of a working party. *Developmental Medicine and Child Neurology*, **6**, 530–535.
KANNER, L. (1943) Autistic disturbances of affective contact. *Nervous Child*, **2**, 217–250.
LOTTER, V. (1966) Epidemiology of autistic conditions in young children: I. Prevalence. *Social Psychiatry*, **1**, 124–137.
RIMLAND, B. (1968) On the objective diagnosis of infantile autism. *Acta Paedopsychiatrica*, **35**, 146–161.
—— (1971) The differentiation of childhood psychoses: an analysis of checklists for 2218 psychotic children. *Journal of Autism and Childhood Schizophrenia*, **1**, 161–174.
RUTTER, M. (1978) Diagnosis and definition in childhood autism. *Journal of Autism and Childhood Schizophrenia*, **8**, 139–161.
WING, L. (1981) Asperger's syndrome: a clinical account. *Psychological Medicine*, **11**, 115–129.
—— & GOULD, J. (1979) Severe impairments of social interaction and associated abnormalities in children: epidemiology and classification. *Journal of Autism and Developmental Disorders*, **9**, 11–29.
WORLD HEALTH ORGANIZATION (1977) *International Classification of Diseases: Ninth Revision*. Geneva: WHO.
—— (1987) *International Classification of Diseases: Tenth Revision Draft: Research Diagnostic Criteria*. Geneva: WHO (unpublished document).

1 Autism: possible clues to the underlying pathology—1. Clinical facts

LORNA WING

When Kanner (1943) first described the cluster of features he called autism, he speculated on possible causes. He was half inclined to a genetic aetiology, but he also suggested that abnormal child-rearing practices by parents with high academic attainments and abnormal personalities were responsible for the children's strange behaviour. In the climate of the time, this became the most widely known hypothesis. With advances in knowledge of autism and of neuropathology views have changed, but the old ideas are still to be found in some clinics, causing much unhappiness to parents and inappropriate treatment of affected children. For this reason, it was decided that the introductory talks for this conference should set the scene by presenting reasons why detailed knowledge of autism from the medical, psychological and parental points of view strongly suggests a physical cause.

Population studies

Studies of prevalence within whole populations living in defined geographical areas are essential in the process of building up understanding of any clinical condition. Theories developed on the basis of small numbers of diagnosed cases seen in one particular clinic are likely to be subject to error due to biases in referrals. Kanner's original work on 11 autistic children was affected by such problems, and epidemiological studies have played an important part in setting the record straight.

The first large-scale population study was carried out by Lotter (1966, 1967). He established the prevalence of autism in the former English county of Middlesex as 4.5 per 10 000 children.

Wing & Gould (1979) examined the prevalence of autism in children in the former London borough of Camberwell. They used Lotter's definition to find the syndrome in typical form (see the Preface), but they also looked for all children with any of the features of behaviour described as occurring in autism, whether or not the full typical picture was present and whatever

TABLE I
Camberwell population study

| | Children aged 0–14 on 31.12.70 | | |
IQ on standardised tests	'Typical' autism	Any autistic features	No autistic features
0–19 (profound retardation)	✓	✓	✓
20–49 (severe retardation)	✓	✓	✓
50–69 (mild retardation)	✓	✓	—
70 + (normal)	✓	✓	—

✓ = included in study
— = included *only* if in services for severe mental retardation (because functioning as severely retarded in everyday skills)

the child's intelligence quotient (IQ). In addition, they included all children who were functioning as severely mentally retarded, whether or not they showed autistic features (see Table I).

Altogether, 173 out of a total population of 35 000 children aged under 15 years were eligible for the study, but 7 died or were otherwise lost before they could be assessed. From the remaining 166 children, 17 (4.9 per 10 000) were identified as having typical autism. However, a further 73 were found also to have impairments of social interaction, communication and imagination (referred to as the 'triad' of impairments), plus a repetitive stereotyped pattern of activities, as defined in the Preface, although they did not fit the full picture of typical autism. The whole group, including those with autism, is conceptualised as the 'autistic continuum' (or spectrum) and appears to be roughly equivalent to the group of Pervasive Developmental Disorders as defined in the American Psychiatric Association's (1987) *Diagnostic and Statistical Manual of Mental Disorders* (3rd edn — revised) (DSM–III–R). Wing & Gould' autistic continuum includes children who are profoundly mentally retarded and non-mobile, as long as they have the triad of impairments. In their study, 17 of the socially impaired group were unable to walk independently.

It should be emphasised that, in the Camberwell study, all the diagnoses were made by the research workers. Only one half of the children with typical autism had been referred to a psychiatrist and identified as autistic, even though there was easy access to clinics with staff who had a special interest in childhood autism.

In the following discussion, the findings for the full autistic continuum will be considered, for two reasons. Firstly, it was not possible to define a clear division between the autistic group and the rest of those with the triad. Secondly, different definitions of 'autism' carve out different though overlapping segments of the continuum, as shown in the Preface. A number of variables were examined in the study subjects, but only those providing evidence relevant to theories of aetiology of autism and related conditions will be mentioned here.

Social class

Social class was determined from the father's (or chief wage-earner's) occupation, using the Registrar-General's fivefold classification. Contrary to Kanner's findings, there was no social class bias among the parents of the autistic children, nor among the parents of the rest of the children in the autistic continuum, when compared with the total population of Camberwell, or with the parents of the sociable severely retarded children (Wing, 1980). This remained the case even when immigrant families (mainly from the Caribbean) were excluded in case there was any tendency towards more manual occupations in this group due to the social disadvantages associated with migration. Thus, the population study did not support Kanner's idea that autistic children had parents with high academic attainments and professional occupations.

A clue to the reason why Kanner found a social class bias came from examination of the parents of children seen by the present author as out-patients, not as participants in the research study. These children came from all over the country, in most cases because the parents themselves had requested referral. In these families there was a marked bias towards higher educational and occupational class, presumably because they were mainly a self-selected group.

Schopler *et al* (1979) and Tsai *et al* (1982) reviewed all the studies of social class in parents of autistic children. As pointed out by Tsai *et al*, most of the studies showing high social class bias were conducted before 1970, and those showing no bias were carried out after that date. This is additional corroboration that earlier work was affected by biases in referral.

Sex ratio

All workers who have looked at sex ratios have reported a higher prevalence among boys, though the exact ratios vary from over 2 to 1 to 4 to 1. In the Camberwell study (Wing, 1981), the overall male to female ratio for all those in the continuum was 2.6 to 1. When different IQ bands were examined, it was seen that the most marked excess of males was in those with IQs over 50, where it was 15 to 1. Among the severely retarded (IQ 20–49) it was 3.5 to 1 and among the profoundly retarded (IQ under 20) it was 1.4 to 1. For the typically autistic group the ratio was very high indeed (16 to 1), but this was probably an artefact of the small numbers. The one girl had an IQ below 50. A marked excess of boys among autistic children with higher levels of intelligence on tests has been noted by other authors (Lotter, 1966; Tsai *et al*, 1981; Lord *et al*, 1982).

It would be difficult to explain the marked excess of boys and the IQ-related differences in sex ratios on a psychogenic hypothesis. The evidence gradually accumulating suggests that autism can result from a variety of different physical causes, among which sex-linked genetic factors may play a part (see Chapter 5).

Among sociable severely retarded children there was a slight excess of boys, the ratio being 1.2 to 1.

Mental retardation

Mental retardation (IQ below 70) was closely associated with the triad of social impairments (Wing & Gould, 1979), as shown in Table II.

Those with typical autism were somewhat more likely to be of higher IQ than the rest of the autistic continuum. This is not surprising, since one of the criteria is the presence of complex repetitive routines, which need some visuo-spatial ability for their performance. Nevertheless, the majority of the autistic children had IQs in the 20–49 range, even using tests based on visuo-spatial skills not involving language. The full picture of typical autism is rare among the profoundly retarded (IQ 0–19), but, in the Camberwell study, nearly one half of those with the triad who were not typically autistic were in the profoundly retarded range. A high proportion of these (44%) were non-mobile.

Conversely, approximately half of all the children with IQs below 50 in the Camberwell study had the triad of social impairments.

In Chapter 3, Uta Frith discusses in detail the pattern of cognitive deficits in socially impaired children and their significance for aetiology. In the present context of findings from epidemiology, it is sufficient to point out that the Camberwell study showed an especially marked association between IQ and the severity of the manifestation of social impairment. The children who were most aloof and indifferent to others, appearing to be completely

TABLE II
IQs of children in the Camberwell study

	'Typical' autism (No. = 17)	Other socially impaired (No. = 73)	All socially impaired (No. = 90)
IQ 0–19: %	6	49[1]	41
IQ 20–49: %	65	26	41
IQ 50–69: %	24	9	14
IQ 70 + : %	6	2	3
Total	100	100	100

[1] Almost half of this group were non-mobile.

in a world of their own, a feature which Kanner considered to be the core of his syndrome, were those who were the most severely or profoundly retarded, and the most likely to have an identifiable physical cause for their handicaps.

A close relationship between autism (however defined) and mental retardation has been reported by many other authors, including Lotter (1966), Lockyer & Rutter (1969), Kolvin *et al* (1971), DeMyer *et al* (1974) and DeMyer (1976).

The Camberwell children, now aged over 16 years, have recently been followed up. All those who were socially impaired as children retained this handicap into adolescence or adult life, even though, in 20%, the way it was manifested changed, for example from aloofness to active but odd approaches (Wing, 1988). Those who were mentally retarded as children remained so as adults, the tendency being for the IQ on testing to remain roughly the same or to fall slightly. Other follow-up studies have also shown the persistence of these handicaps (Rutter, 1970; DeMyer *et al*, 1973).

Physical causes of brain dysfunction

Certain kinds of physical disorder that can cause brain damage or dysfunction have been reported in the literature in association with autism. At the time the first Camberwell study was carried out, these reported disorders included maternal rubella (Wing, 1969, 1971; Chess, 1971); untreated phenylketonuria (Jervis, 1963); tuberose sclerosis (Critchley & Earl, 1932; Earl, 1934); encephalitis and encephalopathy (Greenbaum & Lurie, 1948; Asperger, 1960*a*, *b*); severe perinatal complications (Lotter, 1967; Folstein & Rutter, 1977); severe congenital visual impairments associated with brain damage (Keeler, 1958; Freedman, 1971); and infantile spasms (Taft & Cohen, 1971). On the other hand, the pattern of impairments appeared to be uncommon in children with Down's syndrome (Wing, 1969).

In the Camberwell study, the prevalence of the above conditions was examined in the group with the triad of social impairments and in the sociable severely retarded children. One or more of the conditions listed above were reported in 40% of the socially impaired children, but in only 12% of the sociable severely retarded. In those with typical autism, 47% had one or more of the relevant associated conditions in their history or present state.

When all conditions which could be associated with brain dysfunction were counted, it was found that these were reported in 68% of all children with the triad, and 53% of the subgroup with autism. Of the sociable severely retarded, 85% had identifiable, probably causal, conditions in the history or present state, more than one third of these being Down's syndrome.

As mentioned previously, the most severely or profoundly retarded and the most aloof children were most likely to have an identifiable associated condition which could be of aetiological significance.

Since the first Camberwell study was completed, there has been progress in identifying physical factors that may be associated with autism and related conditions. Work on genetic factors, including fragile X (Chapter 5); biochemical abnormalities (Chapters 6,7, and 8); and newer brain-imaging techniques may give clues to the physical causes of the social impairments in those with higher levels of intelligence in whom the gross aetiology is not identifiable from the history or clinical examination.

The question arises whether typically autistic children without any obvious physical cause for their handicaps differ from those in whom a possible cause can be found. Apart from a tendency for the latter to have lower IQs, no clinical features distinguished the groups. For example, one of the most typically autistic boys in the nuclear group, with an IQ of 90 on visuo-spatial tasks but around 30–40 on language-based tests, was the victim of maternal rubella. Another equally typically autistic boy, with good drawing skills, had had infantile spasms at the age of 6 months. The same kinds of rather complex stereotyped routines, abnormalities of language and social impairments were seen whether or not an obvious associated condition could be identified.

As time goes on, and advances are made in diagnostic techniques, the group with 'unknown aetiology' becomes smaller and smaller and it seems likely that one day it will disappear altogether.

Epilepsy

Epilepsy is a manifestation of brain damage or dysfunction that is common in socially impaired children and adults (Rutter, 1970; Deykin & MacMahon, 1979). Among the children with the triad in the Camberwell study, 48% had had at least one fit at some time during their lives up to the age of follow-up (16–31 years). Two developed fits at the age of 19 years, and more of the group may do so in the future. Among the sociable severely retarded the proportion was 21%.

If the non-mobile children are excluded (17 socially impaired and 12 sociable), 38% of the socially impaired children had had at least one fit at follow-up, compared with 15% of the sociable children. Four of the mobile socially impaired had their first fit as teenagers, compared with one of the sociable group. Among the typically autistic children, 29% had had at least one fit up to the time of follow-up.

As would be expected, fits were more common among those with severe or profound mental retardation. Whereas less than a quarter of the socially impaired with IQ of 50 or over had had a fit, the proportion for those with IQ under 50 was more than a half.

Motor disorders

Kanner's work was of great value in introducing the concept of childhood autism and thereby drawing attention to the existence of impairments of the development of social interaction and empathy. On the other hand, his insistence on the separateness of his syndrome from other disorders was unhelpful. In order to increase understanding of the nature of autism and related conditions it is necessary to see them in the context of other neurological and psychiatric disorders in adults as well as children.

All the clinical phenomena of the autistic continuum — for example, echolalia; repetitive speech; concrete, literal interpretation of language; lack of social interest and empathy; a narrow range of activities and acute distress and anger when these are interrupted; sleep disturbances; excessive intake of fluids and so on — have analogies in other conditions following from identifiable brain damage or dysfunction, including pre-senile and senile dementia. The significance of the language and cognitive problems are discussed in detail by Uta Frith (Chapter 3). In this section, I shall outline one other aspect that does not always receive attention — namely, the disorders of motor function.

Autistic children can give the impression of skilful lively movement, because of a springy walk, often on tiptoes, and an ability to climb and balance without any fear. But this appearance hides a range of problems in gross or fine movements when the children are given tasks to do (DeMyer, 1976). Around adolescence, they tend to become rather clumsy and ill co-ordinated in their movements. This was very evident in the Camberwell follow-up study. It is interesting that the clumsiness is often more obvious in those of higher ability who develop speech. This fits in with the fact that Asperger (1944), who observed and described the more able and verbal people in the autistic continuum during their adolescence, placed such emphasis on their poor co-ordination and lack of common sense in motor as well as other areas.

Odd postures of the body, limbs and hands, which are difficult for normal people to imitate, occur throughout childhood in many of those in the continuum. These problems tend to be exacerbated in adolescence, especially in periods of difficult behaviour. Other phenomena of this kind include becoming temporarily 'frozen' into a posture in the middle of carrying out a task, or attempting over and over again to complete a movement, such as going through a door, but failing unless someone gives a verbal command or a physical push.

Sudden, jerky movements and vocalisations, including recognisable obscenities, occur in some people in the autistic continuum and are strongly reminiscent of the clinical picture of Gilles de la Tourette's syndrome. (Realmuto & Main, 1982).

Some of the motor and other phenomena seen in autistic conditions are similar to those in Parkinsonism following encephalitis, as anyone reading Oliver Sacks' book on the latter condition will have observed (Sacks, 1982).

Speculations about causes

The epidemiological and clinical facts strongly suggest that disorders in the autistic continuum are due to brain damage or dysfunction, but it seems that many different initial causes may each give rise to the abnormal behaviour pattern. Furthermore, autistic spectrum disorders by no means always result from the conditions mentioned. Nevertheless, the high rate of such abnormalities in people with autistic spectrum disorders must be taken seriously. The suggestion that any handicap makes a child emotionally vulnerable to social impairment is not supported by the fact that two conditions involving brain pathology and handicap, namely Down's syndrome and cerebral palsy, are rather unlikely to be associated with autism; and — as shown in the Camberwell study, in which children with any handicap, physical or psychological, were screened — physical handicaps alone do not seem to have any more association with the autistic spectrum than would be expected by chance alone (Wing & Gould, 1979). The most likely hypothesis is that all these different causes need to affect particular brain areas or functions for social impairment to result, and that this occurs under circumstances as yet unknown.

Whether or not a child fits the picture of 'typical' autism will depend upon the severity of the social impairment and the degree and kind of brain dysfunction in other areas. Thus, if a child is aloof and indifferent to people, at least in his early years, and has marked impairment of language skills, but his visuo-spatial abilities are less damaged, he will merit the diagnosis of autism. If he is severely socially impaired and all his other skills are equally damaged, he will be diagnosed profoundly physically and mentally handicapped and the 'autism' will be one more problem on top of the rest. If he is socially impaired but not aloof, and has all or most other skills intact, he is likely to fit Asperger's (1944) description of his syndrome, and so on. Many combinations of impairments will not exactly fit any of the named 'syndromes'. The concept of a 'spectrum of autistic disorders' or the 'triad of social impairments' helps to make sense out of the confusion of clinical facts.

If there is a focus of pathology upon which all the various initial physical causes must act, where is it to be found?

Because of the language problems it has been suggested that the left hemisphere, which in most people deals with formal language, is the specific site (Blackstock, 1978), but this is probably too simplistic a view of the problem (Arnold & Schwartz, 1983).

Ricks & Wing (1975) described the lack of pre-verbal communication in young autistic children, and suggested that such communication was so necessary to the survival of any species that it was likely to be sited in the parts of the brain that, in evolutionary terms, are older, rather than more recently developed. Higher cortical function may of course be affected as a secondary consequence.

Damasio & Maurer (1978) considered the details of the clinical picture in autistic spectrum disorders, including the disturbances of posture and movements, and related them to the consequences of various neuro-logical lesions. They came to the conclusion that the dysfunction is in the phylogenetically older parts of the cortex and the striatum, the variations in the clinical picture among different individuals being related to differences in the precise details of the structures affected within this general area.

It is interesting and useful to speculate on the possible neurological pathology, so long as the ideas are regarded as hypotheses only, until validated by solid evidence. To be taken seriously, any theory of cause must be able to account for all the clinical and epidemiological phenomena, and for the relationship of autism to the rest of the continuum of conditions involving social impairment.

References

AMERICAN PSYCHIATRIC ASSOCIATION (1987) *Diagnostic and Statistical Manual of Mental Disorders* (3rd edn, revised) (DSM-III-R). Washington: APA.

ARNOLD, G. & SCHWARTZ, S. (1983) Hemispheric lateralization of language in autistic and aphasic children. *Journal of Autism and Developmental Disorders*, **13**, 129–140.

ASPERGER, H. (1944) Die autistischen Psychopathen im Kindersalter. *Archiv. für Psychiatrie und Nervenkrankheiten*, **117**, 76–136.

—— (1960a) Infections and mental retardation. In *Mental Retardation: Proceedings of the First International Medical Conference, Portland, Maine* (eds P. Bowman & H. Mautner). New York: Grune & Stratton.

—— (1960b) Behaviour problems and mental retardation. In *Mental Retardation: Proceedings of the First International Medical Conference, Portland, Maine* (eds P. Bowman & H. Mautner). New York: Grune & Stratton.

BLACKSTOCK, E. G. (1978) Cerebral asymmetry and the development of early infantile autism. *Journal of Austism and Childhood Schizophrenia*, **8**, 339–353.

CHESS, S. (1971) Autism in children with congenital rubella *Journal of Autism and Childhood Schizophrenia*, **1**, 33–47

CRITCHLEY, M. & EARL, C. J. C. (1932) Tuberose sclerosis and allied conditions. *Brain*, **55**, 311–346.

DAMASIO, A. R. & MAURER, R. G (1978) A neurological model for childhood autism. *Archives of Neurology*, **35**, 777–786.

DEMYER, M. K. (1976) Motor, perceptual–motor and intellectual disabilities of autistic children. In *Early Childhood Autism* (ed. L. Wing), 2nd edn. Oxford: Pergamon Press.

—— BARTON, S., DEMYER, W. E., NORTON, J. A., ALLEN, J & STEELE. R. (1973) Prognosis in autism: a follow-up study. *Journal of Autism and Childhood Schizophrenia*, **3**, 199–246.

—— BARTON, S., ALPERN, G. D. KIMBERLIN, C., ALLEN, J., YANG, E. & STEELE, R. (1974) The measured intelligence of autistic children. *Journal of Autism and Childhood Schizophrenia*, **4**, 42–60.

DEYKIN, E. Y. & MACMAHON, B. (1979) The incidence of seizures among children with autistic symptoms. *American Journal of Psychiatry*, **136**, 1310–1312.

EARL, C. J. C. (1934) The primitive catatonic psychosis of idiocy. *British Journal of Medical Psychology*, **14**, 230–253.

FOLSTEIN, S. & RUTTER, M. (1977) Infantile autism: a genetic study of 21 twin pairs. *Journal of Child Psychology and Psychiatry*, **18**, 297–322.

FREEDMAN, D. A. (1971) Congenital and perinatal sensory deprivation: some studies in early development. *American Journal of Psychiatry*, **127**, 1539–1545.

GREENBAUM, J. V. & LURIE, L. A. (1948) Encephalitis as a causative factor in behaviour disorders in children: analysis of 78 cases. *Journal of the American Medical Association*, **136**, 923–930.

JERVIS, G. A. (1963) The clinical picture. In *Phenylketonuria* (ed. F. L. Lyman). Springfield, Illinois: Charles C. Thomas.

KANNER, L. (1943) Autistic disturbances of affective contact. *Nervous Child*, **2**, 217–250.

KEELER, W. R. (1958) Autistic patterns and defective communication in blind children with retrolental fibroplasia. In *Psychopathology of Communication* (eds P. H. Hoch & J. Zubin). New York: Grune & Stratton.

KOLVIN, I., HUMPHREY, M. & MCNAY, A. (1971) Studies in the childhood psychoses: VI. Cognitive factors in childhood psychoses. *British Journal of Psychiatry*, **118**, 415–420.

LOCKYER, L. & RUTTER, M. (1969) A five to fifteen year follow-up study of infantile psychosis: III. Psychological aspects. *British Journal of Psychiatry*, **115**, 865–882.

LORD, C., SCHOPLER, E. & REVICKI, D. (1982) Sex differences in autism. *Journal of Autism and Developmental Disorders*, **12**, 317–330.

LOTTER, V. (1966) Epidemiology of autistic conditions in young children: I. Prevalence. *Social Psychiatry*, **1**, 124–137.

—— (1967) Epidemiology of autistic conditions in young children: II. Some characteristics of the parents and children. *Social Psychiatry*, **1**, 163–173.

REALMUTO, G. M. & MAIN, B. (1982) Coincidence of Tourette's disorder and infantile autism. *Journal of Autism and Developmental Disorders*, **12**, 367–372.

RICKS, D. M. & WING, L. (1975) Language, communication and the use of symbols in normal and autistic children. *Journal of Autism and Childhood Schizophrenia*, **5**, 191–221.

RUTTER, M. (1970) Autistic children: infancy to adulthood. *Seminars in Psychiatry*, **2**, 435–450.

SACKS, O. (1982) *Awakenings*, revised edition. London: Pan Books.

SCHOPLER, E., ANDREWS, C. E. & STRUPP, K. (1979) Do autistic children come from upper-middle-class parents? *Journal of Autism and Developmental Disorders*, **9**, 139–152.

TAFT, L. T. & COHEN, H. J. (1971) Hypsarrhythmia and childhood autism: a clinical report. *Journal of Autism and Childhood Schizophrenia*, **1**, 327–336.

TSAI, L., STEWART, M. A. & AUGUST, G. (1981) Implication of sex differences in the familial transmission of infantile autism. *Journal of Autism and Developmental Disorders*, **11**, 165–174.

—— STEWART, M. A., FAUST, M. & SHOOK, S. (1982) Social class distribution of fathers and children enrolled in the Iowa autism program. *Journal of Autism and Developmental Disorders*, **12**, 211–222.

WING, L. (1969) The handicaps of autistic children—a comparative study. *Journal of Child Psychology and Psychiatry*, **10**, 1–40.

—— (1971) Perceptual and language development in autistic children: a comparative study. In *Infantile Autism: Concepts, Characteristics and Treatment* (ed. M. Rutter). London: Churchill.

—— (1980) Childhood autism and social class. *British Journal of Psychiatry*, **137**, 410–417.

—— (1981) Sex ratios in early childhood autism and related conditions. *Psychiatry Research*, **5**, 129–137.

—— (1988) The continuum of autistic characteristics. In *Diagnosis and Assessment in Autism* (eds E. Schopler & G. Mesibov). New York: Plenum Press.

—— & GOULD, J. (1979) Severe impairments of social interaction and associated abnormalities in children: epidemiology and classification. *Journal of Autism and Developmental Disorders*, **9**, 11–29.

2 Autism: possible clues to the underlying pathology—2. A parent's view

PAUL SHATTOCK

Over the years we have seen many theories put forward to explain the occurrence of autism in children. In the earliest publications it was felt that parent's indifference and coolness towards their children was the major contributory factor, but the weight of clinical opinion, in the English-speaking world at least, soon switched to a belief in physical agents as the cause. Recently, however, the earlier ideas have been resurrected (if they ever disappeared) and received much publicity, particularly in the non-specialised press, so causing further anxiety to parents.

The mere fact that we wish something to be true or false does not make it so, and in order to determine the truth in this matter it is necessary to examine all the evidence from all available sources. Scientific literature is pervaded by discussions which enhance the preconceived tenets of the authors, but it is vital that all evidence should be considered, without ruling out the possibility of the unpalatable truth, before final conclusions are reached. If the evidence justifies a conclusion that there is a psychogenic cause for autism, and a portion of 'blame' is put on to parents, this should be the basis for treatment. If the evidence indicates an organic cause for autism, this should be given maximal exposure to eradicate the cruelties inherent in the parent-oriented theories. The cruelty of these explanations lies in the fact that parents already feel guilt through being unable to communicate with their own children, without having the added burden of being branded as the cause of their children's permanent handicap.

Jamie

As the parent of an autistic child, now aged 17, I claim no particular abilites which enable me to pronounce on these matters except an intimate knowledge of the growth and development of one particular autistic boy. Jamie would be classified as autistic using any of the systems for diagnosis described elsewhere in this publication. I feel that my experiences with him constitute a qualification for my making the following observations.

Our story is the same as that of most other parents of autistic children. An apparently normal baby, in our case a particularly well behaved and docile child (which may in itself be significant but is usually ignored), does not develop in quite the expected way as he grows older. We are branded as over-anxious parents and told not to worry. Over the next few years his behaviour becomes so strange, and development, particularly that of language, so patchy, that even 'the experts' are forced to admit that there is a problem. Several years later the diagnosis of autism is given. Before it had time to sink in we read everything we could find on the subject and saw, with great clarity, that this was the problem. It was so obvious. There in black and white were listed the strange behaviours we had seen in our son. The language difficulties; the avoidance of gaze; the obsessive behaviour; the routines; the spinning on the toes; they were all there.

Further study of the literature gave us some sort of explanations for the behaviours, explanations which did not make the condition any less perplexing but which helped us to understand how to handle the difficult situations they generated.

Through our local society and the school which Jamie attends we came into contact with other children and parents and we began to notice similarities in the behaviour of our children. These were often isolated instances of detailed behaviour or actions in addition to the major symptoms described elsewhere.

The pieces of the puzzle

Gradually the professional scientists are piecing together the isolated fragments which make up the jigsaw puzzle of autism, but there may be other pieces lying around whose significance is not yet apparent. Virtually all the research so far reported has concentrated on the psychological or behavioural symptoms of autism, because specialists in these areas first took an interest in our problems. It is likely that there are other, very significant, clues in the physiological processes of the autistic person's body and it is to these that attention is now being turned. It is with this in mind that I wish to bring to the attention of the professionals some of these minor manifestations of autism. These may not be universally present in our children but they do seem to be fairly common. As far as I am aware hard data have not been published to prove their existence, but I include them nevertheless.

Response to pain

There are, in the literature, descriptions of the variability in response to pain which is exhibited by autistic people, and how, on the whole, autistic people do not appear to feel pain as intensely as the rest of us. The same appears to be true for extremes of heat or cold. My son, when engrossed in some task, may totally ignore what should be physically extremely painful stimuli. Sometimes, on the other hand, he may react excessively to some trivial physical offence to his person, crying and wanting comfort because of it. It always seems to me that this reaction is not automatic, as it is in normal children, but is a learned response. He has seen other children cry on such occasions and feels that this is appropriate — perhaps they even received a reward such as a sweet for the behaviour — and so he attempts to do the same. The response appears to be the consequence of logical thought rather than an automatic one.

Stool size

A number of parents have commented on the impressive size of the motions passed by their autistic children. It has also been observed that the motions tend to float. Although no statistical evidence has been produced, the observation was recorded by a parent some years ago; yet its significance remains undiscussed (Sullivan, 1975). Psychological causes are possible; so are disrupted eating patterns; but a chemical influence on gut motility is at least as likely. Workers with mixed groups of 'mentally handicapped' people have confirmed to me personally that they have observed this phenomenon only with their autistic clients.

Temper bouts

A high proportion of autistic children experience temper tantrums of extreme intensity. These seem to be particularly prevalent in the younger age range but they also frequently appear for a period of time, perhaps a year or two, in the early or middle teens, and may well be associated with pubertal changes. In my son, the tantrums were of utter savagery and violence, often directed at loved ones or inanimate objects. It would appear as if he were possessed and it was difficult to believe that it was our son behaving in this way. Trivial events tended to trigger off these attacks, but to me it often appeared that these events were engineered by my son as if he wanted them to happen. It was possible to see an attack coming, but whatever we did to head it off it still happened. It was almost like a fit, as if the fury came from deep within him and he had no control over it.

When the violence was over, the shouting, biting, scratching and spitting gave way slowly to sobbing and apparent remorse, and for the next hour or so Jamie would be exceptionally friendly, amenable, alert and responsive, far more so than usual. It was as if something had been purged from his system. For about 18 months his was a real Jekyll and Hyde existence, with about three attacks a day, lasting an hour or so each time. Considering the known effects of the opioids on pain reception, gut motility and the production of euphoria, it is tempting to speculate upon their involvement in these phenomena.

Although not strictly relevant to this heading, the tendency of a significant proportion of autistic adolescents to begin having epileptic attacks is difficult to reconcile with a psychogenic cause for autism.

Eating habits

There are a number of ways in which the feeding habits of autistic people vary from those of the normal population. Firstly, preparatory to eating food, many autistic people sniff it or test its temperature as if suspicious of some potential harm. The eating process may be preceded by a period of picking bits off the food, but once started may progress at an alarming rate. There appears a distinct although not universal preference for highly flavoured foods. My own son has always been particularly fond of sandwich spread, salad cream and Marmite, all of which he spreads on his bread in heroic quantities, often all at the same time.

His eating habits are not consistent; at times he and other autistic children seem to exist on very little, while on other occasions they may eat ravenously for a period of time. Four eggs, three bowls of cereal and eleven pieces of toast is a rather excessive amount for an 11-year-old's breakfast.

Periodic behaviour patterns

We noticed that, over a considerable period, Jamie's behaviour, mood and physical condition varied markedly. Every six weeks or so he appeared to get a high temperature, go off his food, become listless and irritable, and experience disrupted sleep patterns, so that he would not sleep at night but rested in bed during the day and generally opted out of life. Yet there would be no evidence of infectious disease at this time. Other parents have noted a similar 'feverish' phenomenon (Sullivan, 1975) and reported heightened awareness and better communication at these times. We did not observe this. I understand, however, that this improved behaviour at times of feverishness is not restricted to cases of autism. When Jamie recovered from these periods of feverishness his appetite for food was enormous (see above!).

Effects of medication

There are many drugs which various authorities have described as being useful in the modification of behaviour in autistic people. One cannot be dogmatic in these matters on account of the variability of the effects of drugs on different subjects, but it would seem that, on the whole, our autistic children do not react to medication in quite the same way as the normal population.

For example, chlorpromazine (Largactil) and thioridazine (Melleril) seem to be less effective as tranquillisers than would be expected. Personal observations also suggest an increase in extrapyramidal side effects in our children. Drugs such as haloperidol (Serenace) seemed to make my son totally incapable of keeping still. I can remember walking the beach with him in the early hours of the morning while his eyes rolled right up under his eyelids 15 hours after a single dose of droperidol. This was in spite of other drugs to take away the side-effects. Both of these effects appear to occur in brain-damaged mentally handicapped children and not just in those with autism. This provides further support for an organic cause for autism.

Perimeters

One of the unrecorded (as far as I am aware) activities of a proportion of autistic children is to prowl around the perimeters of any space in which they are enclosed or feel enclosed. A fair proportion of them will expend much effort in pressing against enclosing perimeters, whether they be walls around a room, hedges around a field or barriers in a street. On numerous occasions our son has had to be retrieved from the stock rooms of shops where his boundary-determining experiments have taken him.

I can offer no rational explanation for this behaviour. Could it be the surfacing of some normally suppressed territorial ritual? Could it be a physical expression of his attempts to determine his mental boundaries or limitations? Could it just be a fun thing to do?

Other observations

There are a number of other observations which have been brought to my attention during the preparation of this piece, but although suggested by people closely involved with autism and potentially of great significance, I have found no corroborative evidence. I therefore ask the questions: Do autistic people suffer less infectious disease than their normal counterparts? Do autistic people experience increased intestinal disorders, for example diarrhoea and flatulence? Do autistic people have goose pimples more frequently than normal people? Do autistic people tend to have smaller pupils than the normal population?

Personal accounts

Parents are experts on autism due to their unique exposure to autistic subjects over many years, but there are even better witnesses to the effect of autism and these are the subjects themselves. We are fortunate that a number of autistic people have developed to such an extent that they are able and willing to record their recollections, which give us an important insight into the thoughts of an alert mind which is imprisoned by the difficulties of autism.

For example, David Miedzianik's autobiography (Miedzianik, 1986) makes us aware of life's problems for an intelligent, sensitive autistic person. Temple Grandin's thought-provoking book (Grandin & Scariano, 1986) demonstrates the logicality of the autistic person's behaviour within the context of their own interpretation of the world and its events.

The most recent report, by Darren White (White, 1987), actually describes the distortion of the senses, both visual and auditory, which he experienced. He explains how because of the 'tricks' his ears played on him he was often able to understand the first few words of a sentence but that the rest of the words merged into an incomprehensible mass. He recalls that his vision and hearing could, in his childhood, be likened to an 'untuned television'.

Describing the acquisition of a new bicycle which he received for Christmas he says:

> 'I would not look at it. Extra red was added to the colour making it look orange and it blurred upwards making it look like it was on fire. My favourite colours were those I could see more clearly than others. I also couldn't see blue clearly, it looked too light and it looked like ice. (Imagine the sea on a sunny day, it would look frozen over, in spite of the sun.) The bike was painted purple which I liked better because I could see it more clearly.'

Many parents, although not expressing it in these terms, feel that for some reason or other there is incomplete transmission of data from the sense organs (eyes, ears, taste buds, etc.) to the interpretive centres of the brain, or else that there are faults in the centres themselves. I can imagine that running water would appear to an autistic person not as a colourless, rather boring fluid passing from one place to another but, catching the reflections of light, it would seem to be an endlessly moving pattern of lights and therefore absolutely fascinating and enchanting. The brain will try to make sense of the stimuli it receives in terms of its own experience in rather the same way that we try to make a story out of the disconnected images which make up our dreams. The consequence would be a rather distorted view of the world, as described by White. He also describes auditory distortions, for example, 'Sometimes when people talked it sounded like balloons going off' and 'Once when I was at a mother and baby club I didn't like it because of all the people talking and it sounded like thunder.'

When all the senses, including those for pain and touch, are being modified or adjusted in this way, it is hardly surprising that the world is a very frightening and threatening place for a young autistic person. It is hardly surprisingly that they shun all contact with their fellow human beings and seek solace in safe, repetitive behaviours and routines.

'My child does that'

The above observations, as has been stated already, are based not upon the collection of verified data but upon random observations made by parents and friends of autistic people. It is dangerous, therefore, to treat any of these possible abnormalities as facts, but it is interesting to note how often, when discussing these features with parents, they will say, 'That's right! My child does that.' Each feature individually, as with the other major characteristics of autism, may be liable to some other explanation, but it is unreasonable to admit of anything other than physical cause or causes for the whole spectrum of behaviours and activities which characterise the autistic syndrome.

The relationship between researchers and parents

We parents are grateful for the effort expended by busy professionals on our problems. The studies may be sociological, educational, medical or biochemical, but although few definite answers have been obtained the increasing interest in our problems is most encouraging. It is difficult to estimate exactly how many research-based projects are being carried out throughout the world, but the Autism Research Unit at Sunderland Polytechnic is aware of 37 projects currently under way in the UK. In addition, there are numerous studies carried out by undergraduate students in many disciplines, and attempts to evaluate and educate our children are being carried out in our schools. All of these studies depend upon the co-operation of parents and children to obtain results, so although many of these studies may seem to parents to be rather tiresome and time-consuming, it is vital that we as parents co-operate in every possible way.

On behalf of parents I would request a degree of understanding from researchers that ours is a difficult lot, so that an occasional lapse in enthusiasm for yet another survey, whose significance may, to the parent, be difficult to determine, is sometimes forgivable. Could I suggest, in addition, that researchers do listen to parents. It was, after all, the chance observation of the parent of a child with phenylketonuria which provided the key to solving this problem. Opportunities for contact between research workers and parents should be welcomed and encouraged wherever possible if progress towards the unravelling of the autistic problem is to continue at an ever-increasing rate.

References

GRANDIN, T. & SCARIANO, M. M. (1986) *Emergence Labelled Autistic*. Novato, California: Arena Press.

MIEDZIANIK, D. (1986) *My Autobiography.* Child Development Research Unit, University of Nottingham.
SULLIVAN, R. C. (1975) Hunches on some biological factors in autism. *Journal of Autism and Childhood Schizophrenia,* **5**, 177–184.
WHITE, D., WHITE, B. B. & WHITE, M. S. (1987) Autism from the inside. *Medical Hypotheses,* **24**, 223–229.

3 Autism: possible clues to the underlying pathology—3. Psychological facts

UTA FRITH

The search for the biological basis of autism has gathered momentum at all levels—from molecular genetic structures to physiological or anatomical brain systems. It is already clear that autism can be due to a large variety of causes. Presumably, each of these causes compromises normal development and leads to malfunction of one particular brain system. This is sometimes described as the 'final common pathway'. From my point of view it is not enough to establish the identity of this system, but, in addition, it is necessary to show how a particular brain abnormality might relate to the actual symptoms presented by autistic children. Clearly, there is a huge gap between ideas on behavioural symptoms and psychological processes on the one hand, and ideas on the brain and biological processes on the other. Nevertheless, we can ask the question: What clues are there from psychological facts to the underlying pathology of autism?

There is now no doubt that autism implies brain impairment. The evidence from psychological tests is starkly convincing: mental subnormality afflicts the vast majority of autistic children. Those autistic children who are not retarded nevertheless show specific cognitive dysfunction. Both general mental retardation and specific dysfunction are signs of brain pathology.

In contrast, no evidence has been found for psychogenic factors. Apparently, such factors play no role at all in causing pervasive developmental disorders. Psychogenically caused disorders, if anywhere, might be expected in rare and distressing cases of rejected and severely socially deprived children. Skuse (1984) reviewed such cases, and concluded that the damage done to social, emotional and cognitive development does not necessarily result in lasting effects. In no case has autism, either as a symptom or as a syndrome, been a consequence. The strongest implication of this research is that 'most human characteristics . . . are resistant to obliteration by even the most dire early environments'.

Beyond the demonstration of 'organic' signs, are there more specific clues from psychological investigations? Psychometric tests and neuropsychological

19

interpretations have led to equivocal conclusions, and information-processing approaches too have been suggestive rather than conclusive. It seems to me that in order to link behavioural symptoms and biological factors, we need to build bridges in a step-by-step process. A guide for this enterprise is provided by a developmental framework. Here, too, we need to link surface behaviour and underlying biological mechanisms. Links consist of prerequisites for the emergence of normal behaviour. These prerequisites include environmental input and learning, but also innate structures that make it possible that learning takes place, and indeed guarantee that learning is effortless. With this approach we can trace developmental contingencies and thus project a causal chain between surface behaviour and its origins.

I propose that there are some mandatory links in such a chain. From surface *behaviour* we infer the existence of certain underlying psychological *processes*. From the operation of the processes we infer the existence of even deeper underlying enabling *mechanisms*. These mechanisms are innate and require biological explanation. Developmental disorder would arise when a particular prerequisite is missing. Ideally, we would pinpoint the precise mechanism, a fault in which would lead to specific processing deficits, and these would explain the actual symptoms of autism. The faulty mechanism could then be related to a faulty biological process. This is still a task for the future. We cannot simply jump across the gap that exists between brain and behaviour.

Psychological abilities

Psychologists have developed an impressive number of tests of all kinds of behaviour — language, motor skills, memory, sensory perception, reading, spelling and many more. Prominent amongst these tests are intelligence test batteries. Information gained in the standardised test situation makes comparable the work of different investigators, and for that reason alone it is extremely valuable. Above all, however, the information allows comparisons with normative data. Thus, we can say how well an average child of a certain age is expected to do on, say, a vocabulary test. The performance of autistic children has been systematically investigated by means of standardised tests, and this has established a host of important facts which have resulted in a rich and reliable picture of the pattern of abilities.

What the information does not provide is an immediate interpretation of the pattern of abilities in terms of underlying cognitive processes. This is because test performance and underlying processes do not map on to each other in a neat one-to-one relationship. It is very rare that failure in a particular test can be traced to failure in one particular underlying process only.

One intelligence test, the Wechsler Intelligence Scales for Children (WISC), has been used systematically with, by now, many different samples of autistic children. Even though there is variation in test performance from one individual to another, there is nevertheless a highly characteristic pattern of subtest performance that is found throughout the IQ range (e.g. Lockyer & Rutter, 1970; DeMyer, 1975; Tymchuk *et al*, 1977). The lowest performance is associated with the subtest Comprehension, the highest with the subtest known as Block Design, considered to tap spatial ability. Rote memory is often another performance peak, but this appears to be subject to greater variation. The highs and lows in performance are often so far apart in individual subtests that taking averages would be quite misleading! Nothing like such big differences are encountered in normal populations. They constitute an important clue to underlying pathology. But what is the nature of this pathology? Are there abilities that are subject to brain damage, and others that are spared? Or, could it be that cognitive processes are disordered in such a way that performance may be enhanced in certain conditions, but impaired in others?

Amitta Shah is currently investigating the pattern of abilities and in particular the nature of visuo-spatial abilities in autistic children. This study has already shown that it would be wrong to equate performance on a particular test, namely Block Design, with underlying competence in spatial ability. Instead, performance on this test is shown to be dependent on the additional operation of the ability to segment coherent patterns into constituent elements. As proposed by Frith (1985), autistic children can be assumed to show a degree of detachment from normally powerful context effects. Context effects create a particular form of coherence for stimulus arrays. They are, for instance, responsible for the near invisibility of embedded figures. Shah & Frith (1983) found that autistic children can spot embedded figures more easily than their non-autistic peers. In the Block Design test, the pattern to be copied needs to be segmented into elements corresponding to blocks. These elements are effectively hidden figures due to pattern coherence. If autistic children are not subject to strong coherence effects, then segmentation should present no problem. Preliminary results suggest that this may be the case. This may be the reason for the often superior performance on Block Design.

This then is an example of a particular cognitive dysfunction that might explain symptomatic behaviour.

Can the same dysfunction, i.e. context detachment, also explain comprehension impairment and the curious rote memory feats of many autistic children? Why is it that they appear to remember every turn of phrase, but not the gist of a story? According to the hypothesis, it would be assumed that words, the elements of utterances, are similar to embedded figures. Utterances normally create strong coherence between elements. This coherence is experienced as the meaning of an utterance. Without meaning we do not comprehend. It is well known that meaning also influences recall. If this influence were weak, then recall for meaning would be poor. By contrast, verbatim recall, or memory for meaningless and incoherent stimuli, would seem to be relatively superior.

Of course, other interpretations of the pattern of abilities of autistic children are possible, and no final answer has yet been obtained. Nevertheless, it is unlikely that 'rote memory' or 'spatial ability' will turn out to be basic units that correspond to intact and localisable brain functions in an otherwise damaged system.

The possibility of a cognitive deficit in autistic children that would explain their behaviour has been considered since the pioneering work of Hermelin & O'Connor, which they summarised in their monograph in 1970. One idea behind this hypothesis was that deficits identified in experimentally controlled tests implicate specific neurological dysfunction. Thus, it was important that other irrelevant explanations of task failure had to be ruled out. These include, for instance, too low a level of general ability, lack of co-operation, distractability, lack of motivation, extreme timidity in test situations, and problems in comprehension. Hence, a particular methodology had to be developed. In particular, autistic children had to be compared with non-autistic children of the same level of ability relevant to the task in question. Furthermore, tasks had to be found that were known to be congenial to the children, such as jigsaw puzzles, or immediate echoing of speech. Thus, in all experiments a condition was included which allowed autistic children to show equal or superior performance to comparison groups. Thus, the point in investigating cognitive dysfunction is not to demonstrate poor performance but qualitatively different performance.

The studies resulted from this approach (e.g. Hermelin & O'Connor, 1970; Frith, 1972) succeeded in identifying specific cognitive dysfunction in autistic children from the middle range of Wing's autistic continuum. Over and above mental retardation, there were certain peculiarities in the way information was processed. Briefly, there was less recoding of information than would be expected on the basis of the capacity to handle information. Thus, information was received and faithfully transmitted, but without much regard to its meaning. Normally, the meaning of the message exerts a strong effect on the way it is transmitted: memory may be enhanced, or else the information may be changed to conform with the perceived meaning.

Perfect echo-like recall, and perfect photo-like drawing are extraordinary achievements of some autistic individuals. In fact, these high achievements are also signs of specific cognitive abnormality. The performance is different in nature, not just in degree, from that found in normally developing children.

The hypothesis of underlying impairment in information processing has not yet been tested out on the whole range of autistic spectrum disorders. The high IQ range is a notable omission. However, the hypothesis can go a long way towards explaining the typical scatter of abilities on psychological tests. It is another question to what extent it can also account for the cardinal symptoms of autism, namely profound failure in social interaction and communication. The possibility cannot be ruled out that the information processing deficits are quite separate, or are themselves consequences of even deeper underlying cognitive deficits. We only know we have reached the ground when we can postulate a primitive mechanism which explains the process in question. It is from there that we can start to think about biological factors.

Neuropsychological interpretations

Patients with known brain lesions show a cost in depressed level of intelligence test performance. In addition, however, they often show a marked scatter of performance in various subtests of the standard intelligence scales. Relationships between site of lesion and scatter can be traced. For instance, a dip in the performance on certain verbal tests is often thought to be associated with left hemisphere lesions.

Autistic children, too, show a pronounced scatter of scores in tests such as the Wechsler Intelligence Scales. The fact that there is such a scatter, and that it is true for individual cases, not just for groups of cases, is just what one would expect when there is brain dysfunction. Can parallels be drawn between the typical scatter and that shown by neurological patients?

Fein *et al* (1984) have comprehensively reviewed investigations that draw such parallels. These authors discuss the large number of often conflicting studies, and point out that conflicts are almost certainly due to variation in diagnostic criteria. Different populations of autistic children may well have come from different sections of Wing's continuum. This is a serious problem, especially if children are included who suffer from additional problems resulting from more extensive brain damage than the minimum necessary for autism to occur. Fein *et al* conclude that the hypothesis of left hemisphere damage as a specific cause of autism has very little support. Nevertheless, some autistic children, in addition to autism, also suffer from specific left hemisphere impairment. Others might show right hemisphere impairment, and many, bilateral impairment. Entirely consistent with this idea are the results of a subtype analysis based on psychometric test performance (Fein *et al*, 1985). However, regardless of these arguments, a large number of neuropsychological studies, including studies of handedness, provide evidence of as yet unidentified early brain damage that is specific to autism, and that appears to hold throughout Wing's continuum.

A few studies may serve as examples. Jones & Prior (1985) found that mildly and moderately retarded autistic children showed definite signs of neurological dysfunction, for instance, impaired ability to imitate movements. This result is consistent with DeMyer's earlier work (e.g. 1975), which is discussed in an excellent review (DeMyer *et al*, 1981) of ten years of research in autism.

Rumsey (1985) found that very able autistic people showed excessive perseveration tendencies on the Wisconsin card-sorting test. Again, this is an unequivocal sign of neuropsychological dysfunction, and it is clearly independent of general level of ability.

Fein *et al* (1981) found brainstem abnormalities when measuring auditory evoked potentials in autistic children. This is consistent with various other studies suggesting non-specific subcortical dysfunction. What is particularly interesting, however, is that only those children with the most classic symptoms of autism showed the abnormalities. Again, this was independent of level of general ability.

There are a substantial number of electrophysiological studies of autistic children. There is much information on automatic functioning, in terms of heart rate and skin conductance, as well as information on evoked potentials to auditory or visual stimuli. James & Barry (1980) provide a thorough review of such studies. One can conclude that autistic children invariably show either neurological immaturity or pathology. For instance, compared with non-autistic retarded children, autistic children show a lack of habituation to novel stimuli. This could be for a variety of reasons, one of them being chronically high arousal. Other reasons include a failure to distinguish novel from old, perhaps because of a failure to build appropriate memory representations of the stimulus. From this example, it is clear that electrophysiological measures remain ambiguous: they may be part of a primary abnormality, but equally they may be a secondary consequence of another abnormality, possibly faulty information processing. Evidence from neuropsychological studies leads again and again to the conclusion that brain pathology is present in autistic children, but does it tell us where the pathology might be?

Can one make direct links from neuropsychology test performance to underlying cognitive process, and from cognitive process to brain process? I have already given examples that show that it is extraordinarily difficult to disentangle which cognitive processes might be implicated in test performance. Indeed, most tests that are sensitive to neurological damage involve a large number of cognitive processes. To identify any one of them requires lengthy and rigorously controlled experimental work. This is rare.

If patients with neurological disorders are grouped together according to performance deficits on neuropsychological tests, there is no guarantee that their deficits are due to the same kind of neurological problem. This is because failure in a test can be due to many reasons. Clearly, this subgrouping methodology is not to be advocated for autism either. Furthermore, localisation of any brain damage in autism cannot be established by analogy with patients with known brain damage. Instead, we must first approach the problem of defining the critical psychological processes that give rise to the cardinal symptoms of autism. We can then work out appropriate tests that will give us the necessary behavioural evidence. Ideally, we would make novel predictions about behaviour. This would provide a convincing test of the appropriateness of the hypothesised psychological process.

However, a step in the opposite direction also has to be taken. From the hypothesis of a deficit in some underlying process, we must consider how to explain this process in terms of a primitive mechanism. From there we can start to think of anatomical and physiological functions. It is dangerous to jump straight from surface behaviour, however well observed, to physiological explanation. This, then, is the reason that we cannot make much use of existing neuropsychological data.

Representation and metarepresentation

Since autism is a developmental disorder, a model of normal development is needed to provide a framework for explaining the impairments shown by autistic children (Frith, 1987). One of the most recent and most significant advances in conceptualising early development has been made by my colleague, Alan Leslie, He has been concerned with the necessity of explaining the marked increase in mental powers that occurs when a child moves from infancy to early childhood. This increase is reflected in a striking change in play behaviour. After first showing only straightforward play with objects, e.g. rattling a rattle, banging a drum or rolling a wheeled toy, the child begins to show pretend play, e.g. pouring non-existing tea into a container for a cup, and offering it to a doll to sip. Throughout childhood, imaginative play of this kind can be observed. The strange feature of pretend play is that sensory experience and memory for objects and events is blatantly ignored or contradicted. However, it is only from the second year of life that children show this type of play. It is doubtful if young animals show it, and even primates seem to show it rarely, if ever (Premack, 1986).

Alan Leslie suggests (1987) that the increase in cognitive power is due to a primitive mechanism that, though innate, comes into operation only late in infancy. Nevertheless, there are many cognitive skills present already. The child comes into the world equipped with many already functioning cognitive mechanisms. These enable the young infant to learn much about the surrounding physical and social world. A normal infant's knowledge is impressive. In particular, there are mental representations of familiar people, objects and events. However, there are no metarepresentations, i.e. representations of representations. To make it possible for representations themselves to become the object of higher order representations requires a special mechanism. This is the key to an extraordinary advance in development. Leslie suggests that the way in which this might happen is by 'decoupling' primary representations from the real ty of the outer world that they refer to. Decoupled representations can then be made to refer to the reality of the inner world.

Let me give an example: IT IS RAINING. Let this be a representation that truthfully encodes a fact in the real world. It actually is raining. Now, let us 'decouple' it. This is simple. All we need to do is to say it with raised eyebrows, or to put it in quotes. 'IT IS RAINING.' The expression now no longer refers to a state of affairs in the real world. In the outside world, it may or may not be raining. We now place the decoupled expression in relation to the inner world of mental states. Simple enough; we add a mental state verb. John *thinks* 'IT IS RAINING', or, Let's *pretend* 'IT IS RAINING.'

What language expressions do in this simple yet effective way is just what Leslie's mechanism must be doing. If we assume that this is the case, then we have a surprisingly simple explanation of the strange and sudden appearance of pretence: the ability to form metarepresentations. Leslie's mechanism, once available, opens for the child a new world of learning and experience. Alone in play, for instance, there is abundant opportunity for social learning in imitation and role play. However, pretend play is not all that this mechanism allows one to do. It allows one to reflect on thought itself. This, of course, is tantamount to self-awareness. I can't resist here quoting Descartes' famous claim 'cogito ergo sum'. Clearly, what he meant was 'I know I think, therefore I am.'

In the social world of human beings there is a special application for metarepresentations. Not only can the young child represent: MUMMY IS PLEASED WITH ME, but he can comprehend easily the following: MUMMY THINKS I am a good boy (and that is why she is pleased)— even though I have been naughty, but Mummy does not know this yet. Imagine trying to understand this thought without the ability to know what it means that people think, and that thoughts can be different from person to person. It is quite obvious that it is also thanks to the decoupling mechanism that we can lie and deceive each other. What might be less obvious is that teasing and irony are consequences of the same mechanism. Just as in pretence the child knows simultaneously that something is really the case yet not the case (the stick is a stick, yet a horse), so in irony the point is to say the opposite of what one is ostensibly conveying ('. . . and Brutus is an honourable man').

In what way is Leslie's theory of pretence relevant to autism? Let me reiterate that autism is a developmental disorder and that it must be explained as an abnormality of development. What I have in mind is a model of development that incorporates the possibility of arrest at critical points on its course. Leslie's decoupling mechanism, when it becomes operational, defines such a critical point. It corresponds to a quantum leap in cognitive capacity. Furthermore, it enables exactly that type of knowledge and skill to be acquired that is the essence of advanced social communication. It seems to me that arrest at or before this point would lead to the consequences for development that we see in autism.

Wing & Gould's (1979) triad of impairments in social interaction, communication and pretend play can be explained simply by the inability to form or to understand metarepresentations.

Theory of mind

To bring together pretence, deception and irony in terms of a common origin means seeing a new relationship between some of the most typical autistic behaviours. It has long been known that even very able autistic children do not show pretend play, do not lie, and do not understand irony. However, there was no reason to see them as anything but separate impairments, arising independently from failure in imitation learning, social incompetence, and language problems.

One type of behaviour that also originates from the decoupling mechanism had not previously been considered in autistic children. And no wonder, since as behaviour it did not even have a name — until the term 'mentalising' was coined (Morton, 1986). It is simply something that we take totally for granted. If autism really were due to an inability to deal with metarepresentations (this being due to a fault in the decoupling mechanism), then autistic children would not show this behaviour. We thus have a test of our hypothesis.

What mentalising refers to is the ability to reflect on one's own thoughts, and also the ability to think about other people's thoughts. In other words, it is the ability to conceive of other people and of oneself as having a mind. Once this concept is developed we can understand people's behaviour in terms of what they think, feel or believe, not just in terms of what is the case in the real world. In many cases, the actual state of affairs in the world does not determine behaviour, but rather what a person *thinks* or believes is the state of affairs. As an illustration we can look at the following experimental paradigm, invented by Heinz Wimmer and Josef Perner (1983). Simon Baron-Cohen, Alan Leslie and myself used this particular version, called the Sally/Ann experiment (1985). We tested the hypothesis that even able autistic children would show an impairment in mentalising, in contrast to young normal and to Down's syndrome children.

The experiment goes as follows:
Here is Sally
Here is Ann
Sally has a basket
Ann has a box
Sally puts a marble into her basket
Now Sally goes out for a walk
(— She disappears under the table)
Ann — naughty Ann! — takes the marble out of the basket and puts it into her box
(The box is turned upside down)
Sally is coming back from her walk and wants to play with the marble
(Now the critical question is asked:)
Where will Sally look for her marble?
The answer is, of course, in the basket, because this is where Sally put the marble before going out. This is entirely obvious to normal children

by the time they are four, and to most (i.e. 80% of) Down's syndrome children with a mental age of five.

They point to the basket *where Sally thinks the marble is.* They can also tell where the marble really is. In any case, they start giggling as soon as 'naughty' Ann transfers the marble.

In contrast, most autistic children (80%) with a mental age of nine fail this task. They point to the box *where the marble really is.* On questioning, they also remember that Sally put it in the basket in the first place, and that Sally wasn't there when Ann transferred it. What they fail to do is to predict Sally's behaviour on the basis of Sally's belief—which is of course a mental state. Instead, they predict Sally's behaviour on the basis of a physical state of affairs.

We have now replicated this experiment with real people as actors, rather than dolls, and have obtained the same result (Leslie & Frith, 1988). We also obtained similar results using quite different experimental paradigms. We found that the same autistic children who show difficulties in mentalising show no difficulties in understanding physical cause and effect and simple behavioural routines (Baron-Cohen *et al*, 1986). In other words, we demonstrated a dissociation between representations and metarepresentations. It is only metarepresentations, not primary representations, that we have to assume to be weak or absent in autistic children.

From cognitive mechanism to brain system

The causal chain from cognitive mechanism to process and from process to behaviour has more gaps than it has links. Nevertheless, we have at least the plans for a few bridges. It is encouraging that the three primary behavioural symptoms of autism, namely autistic aloneness, failure of verbal and non-verbal communication, and failure to engage in pretend play, can be accounted for at one stroke. Of course, the behaviour that these symptoms imply still needs to be analysed in more detail. Studies of play, of communication and affectionate interpersonal relationships all deserve careful investigation in both autistic and non-autistic children. The cognitive processes underlying these behaviours, too, need exploration. Clearly, there is more to a fully developed theory of mind than a primitive enabling mechanism. Cultural and other environmental factors, as well as constitutional and temperamental factors, will undoubtedly contribute to the development of the concept of other minds and at the same time to the development of self-awareness. Nevertheless, the innate primitive mechanism that Alan Leslie suggested remains the crucial component, without which learning what it is to have a mind would be a gigantic effort.

What primitive mechanisms are for is to make learning effortless. The domain where learning occurs will not be accidental, but of evolutionary significance. The physiologist Barlow (1979), speculating on the survival value of self-consciousness, has this to say:

'Nature has constructed our brains so that, first, we seek to preserve individual consciousness; second, we can only achieve it in real discourse or rehearsed future discourse; and third, important new decisions require the sanction of consciousness. These three aspects of consciousness generate a communal culture in the light of which individual decisions tend to be made. Thus the survival value of consciousness consists of the peculiar form of gregarious behaviour it generates in man; it is Nature's trick to chain him to the herd.'

To explain the decoupling mechanism in terms of other than biologically innate structures would be a hopeless task. But how can we begin to speculate about a biological basis for the decoupling mechanism? There are three possible pointers: the biological structure needed is not found below primate level; it matures relatively late; and it may be the 'final common pathway' that shows dysfunction in all autistic individuals and only in those individuals who show the impairments of Wing's triad.

Are there any suggestions?

References

BARLOW, H. (1979) Nature's joke: a conjecture on the biological role of consciousness. In *Consciousness and the physical world* (eds B. D. Josephson & V. S. Ramachandran). Oxford: Pergamon.

BARON-COHEN, S., LESLIE, A. & FRITH, U. (1985) Does the autistic child have a 'theory of mind'? *Cognition*, 21, 37–46.

——, —— & —— (1986) Mechanical, behavioural and intentional understanding of picture stories in autistic children. *British Journal of Developmental Psychology*, 4, 113–125.

DEMYER, M. K. (1975) The nature of the neuropsychological disability in autistic children. *Journal of Autism and Childhood Schizophrenia*, 5, 109–128.

——, HINTGEN, J. N. & JACKSON, R. K. (1981) Infantile autism reviewed: a decade of research. *Schizophrenia Bulletin*, 7, 388–451.

FEIN, D., SKOFF, B. & MIRSKY, A. F. (1981) Clinical correlates of brainstem dysfunction in autistic children. *Journal of Autism and Developmental Disorders*, 11, 303–315.

——, HUMES, M., KAPLAN, E., LUCCI, D. & WATERHOUSE, L. (1984) The question of left hemisphere dysfunction in infantile autism. *Psychological Bulletin*, 95, 258–281.

——, WATERHOUSE, L., LUCCI, D. & SNYDER, D. (1985) Cognitive subtypes in developmentally disabled children: a pilot study. *Journal of Autism and Developmental Disorders*, 15, 77–95.

FRITH, U. (1972) Cognitive mechanisms in autism: experiments with colour and tone sequence production. *Journal of Autism and Childhood Schizophrenia*, 2, 160–173.

—— (1985) Recent experiments on autistic children's cognitive and social skills. *Communication*, 19, 16–23.

—— (1987) A developmental model for autism. *Colloque INSERM, Vol. 146, Autisme Infantile*, 175–182.

HERMELIN, B. & O'CONNOR, N. (1970) *Psychological experiments with autistic children*. Oxford: Pergamon.

JAMES, A. & BARRY, R. J. (1980) A review of psychophysiology in early onset psychosis. *Schizophrenia Bulletin*, 6, 506–525.

JONES, V. & PRIOR, M. (1985) Motor imitation abilities and neurological signs in autistic children. *Journal of Autism and Developmental Disorders*, 15, 37–46.

LESLIE, A. (1987) Pretense and representation: the origins of a theory of mind. *Psychological Review*, 94, 412–426.

——— & FRITH, U. (1988) Autistic children's understanding of seeing, knowing and believing. *British Journal of Developmental Psychology*, **4**.

LOCKYER, L. & RUTTER, M. (1970) A five to fifteen year follow-up study of infantile psychosis: IV. Patterns of cognitive ability. *British Journal of Social and Clinical Psychology*, **9**, 152–163.

MORTON, J. (1986) Developmental contingency modelling. In *Theory Building in Developmental Psychology* (ed. P. L. L. van Geert). Amsterdam: Elsevier.

PREMACK, D. (1986) *Gavagai! or the Future History of the Animal Language Controversy*. Cambridge, Mass.: MIT Press.

RUMSEY, J. M. (1985) Conceptual problem-solving in highly verbal, nonretarded autistic men. *Journal of Autism and Developmental Disorders*, **15**, 23–36.

SHAH, A. & FRITH, U. (1983) An islet of ability in autistic children: a research note. *Journal of Clinical Psychology and Psychiatry*, **24**, 613–620.

SKUSE, D. (1984) Extreme deprivation in early childhood: II. Theoretical issues and a comparative review. *Journal of Clinical Psychology and Psychiatry*, **25**, 543–572.

TYMCHUK, A. J., SIMMONS, J. O. & NEAFSEY, S. (1977) Intellectual characteristics of adolescent childhood psychotics with high verbal ability. *Journal of Mental Deficiency Research*, **21**, 133–138.

WIMMER, H. & PERNER, J. (1983) Beliefs about beliefs: representation and constraining function of wrong beliefs in young children's understanding of deception. *Cognition*, **13**, 103–128.

WING, L. & GOULD, J. (1979) Severe impairments of social interaction and associated abnormalities in children: epidemiology and classification. *Journal of Autism and Developmental Disorders*, **9**, 11–29.

4 The role of the endogenous opioids in autism and possible relationships to clinical features

CHRISTOPHER GILLBERG

Endogenous opioids are peptides which serve as 'neuroregulators' in the human nervous system. These neuroregulators affect nerve cells in an indirect way by altering the release or action of the 'neurotransmitters', e.g. dopamine, serotonin and epinephrine. Some of the neurotransmitters are currently thought to be crucial in the modulation of various behaviours. Circumstantial evidence for neurotransmitter dysfunction is available in reports on populations and subgroups of patients with infantile autism (IA) (Young *et al*, 1982; Coleman & Gillberg, 1987).

The endogenous opioids, or endorphins, constitute a chemically complex family of peptides. There are three major precursors, each of which is expressed in a separate set of neurons, which in its turn has a unique distribution in the central nervous system (CNS) (Dores *et al*, 1984).

To estimate endorphin activity in autistic patients we are analysing the endorphin contents in the cerebrospinal fluid (CSF). We use a 'receptor assay' technique to tap the biologically active opioids, which, in a procedure called chromatography, are separated into two fractions, fraction I and II.

So far, we have analysed the CSF samples for contents of endorphins in 29 patients diagnosed as suffering from infantile autism. The results partly overlap with those reported in a previous publication on 20 autistic children (Gillberg *et al*, 1985). The purposes of the present study have been twofold:
  (a) to extend the previous study and examine the possibility of an association between autism and endorphin hyperfunction, and
  (b) if possible to find specific clinical correlates of endorphin hyperfunction in autism.

Method

Study groups

Infantile autism (IA)

Twenty-nine infantile autistic children (20 boys and 9 girls), with an age range of 2–13 years (mean 7.0 years, s.d. 2.8 years), participated in the study. They constituted consecutive cases of IA at a university child psychiatric clinic for out- and in-patients in Göteborg, Sweden. All children fulfilled DSM–III (American Psychiatric Association, 1980), Rutter (1978) and Coleman & Gillberg (1985) criteria for IA and had been extensively clinically examined by the author, who contends that they are a fairly representative sample of young children with IA. Several of the children participated in population studies of autism performed in the late 1970s and the early 1980s in and around Göteborg. No particular sampling bias was introduced in the allocation to endorphin analysis, which is currently performed routinely in all new cases of IA.

There was a relatively high rate of epilepsy in the IA group, and eleven children (38%) (five of whom were girls) had suffered at least one major seizure in their lifetime.

Further, five of the boys had the fragile-X syndrome and two of the girls probably had an atypical variant of the Rett syndrome (the *'forme fruste'* (Hagberg & Rasmussen, 1986)). Two children had neurofibromatosis and one had Möbius syndrome.

Ten per cent of the group were of normal intelligence, 35% were mildly mentally retarded, and 55% were diagnosed as suffering from severe mental retardation.

Twenty of the 29 autistic children were included in our previously reported study of endorphin activity in childhood psychosis.

Comparison group H ('healthy')

Comparison group H consisted of eight children (four boys and four girls) who had been examined by the same pediatrician in a pediatric ward because of suspicion of a CNS disorder, which had later been disproved. They were somewhat younger than the autism group (mean 3.2 years, s.d. 2.2 years, range 0.5–6 years).

Comparison group N ('neurological syndrome')

Comparison group N was made up of four cases (two boys and two girls) diagnosed by a neuropediatrician as suffering from a neurological syndrome (three cases of 'uncomplicated' cerebral palsy and one with Hallevorden–Spatz disease). The mean age in this group was 7.8 years (s.d. 5.1 years), with a range of 3–13 years.

Methods used

CSF analysis

Lumbar CSF (2–3 ml) was obtained from each child and kept stored at – 90°C until analysis. Opioid activity was measured in a receptor assay after chromatographic separation of fractions I and II (Terenius & Wahlström, 1975).

Clinical evaluation of the autistic children

Only two of the autistic children were on any kind of medication (both were on anti-epileptic drugs) at the time of the endorphin study. None of the 12 children in the other two groups had drug treatment at the time of the study.

All the autistic children were thoroughly neuropsychiatrically examined by the author, and the mothers (and very often the father too) were interviewed in great detail concerning background factors, development, and behavioural characteristics of the children. All examinations and interviews took place within a month of the endorphin analyses.

Rating of pain sensitivity

All parents underwent detailed questioning about the child's reactions to painful stimuli. Parents were asked, 'How does your child react when given injections, when he or she bruises himself or herself, when he or she hurts himself or herself?' Answers were rated on a five-point scale ranging from 'He or she is very fussy' (1) to 'Reacts very little, never cries' (4) and 'Doesn't seem to react at all or seems to derive pleasure' (5). A score of 4 or 5 was labelled decreased sensitivity to pain.

Rating of self-destructiveness

All parents were asked if the child ever showed self-destructiveness (head-banging, head-hitting, hitting of other parts of body, hair-pulling, biting self, scratching self). Children who had shown episodes (months) of or almost constant self-destructiveness or who showed self-destructiveness at the time of the examination were labelled self-destructive.

Rating of stereotyped motor behaviour

All parents were asked if the child showed 'odd, repetitive movements with the hands, arms, head, body or feet in a highly characteristic fashion without much variation. Typical examples of such movements are hand-flapping, finger mannerisms, head-rolling and body-rocking.' Ratings were made by the author on a five-point scale ranging from 'Almost never shows such movements' (1) to 'Very often shows such movements' (4) and 'Highly typical: constant feature of the child's behaviour repertoire' (5). A score of 4 or 5 was considered as a clear indication of high degree of current stereotypies.

Reliability and validity of ratings concerning
pain sensitivity, self-destructiveness and stereotypies

Eighteen autistic children (nine of whom participated in this study) in the Göteborg region were evaluated by two different raters with regard to pain sensitivity, self-destructiveness and stereotypies. Each child was assessed by the two raters using the questions of the parental questionnaire as the basis for rating. Both raters had known each child for at least a four-month period and were staff members of autism treatment centres. Inter-rater reliability for pain sensitivity, stereotypies (scores of 4 or 5 clustered) and self-destructiveness was excellent, total agreement being reached in 94% (17/18), 83% (15/18) and 100% (18/18) of the cases, respectively.

The parents and staff members agreed in those nine cases assigned to this study. The personnel and the parents had not discussed the issue at any time before completing the questionnaires. Finally, the ratings of pain sensitivity, stereotypies and self-destructiveness were completely 'blind' to the results of the endorphin analysis.

Repeat CSF samples

Four children (all girls, for various reasons) were subjected to repeat lumbar punctures (with an interval of two weeks, one year, 13 months and two years, respectively) and their CSF samples were analysed again for contents of endorphins.

Statistical analyses

Fisher's exact test was used for comparing group means; χ^2 tests with Yates' correction were applied in the comparison of group frequencies. Pearson r coefficients were calculated for some correlation analyses.

Abnormal values

Abnormal levels of endorphin were considered to be present in any child showing values exceeding the mean + 2 standard deviations of comparison group H.

Results

Endorphin fraction I levels

Seven of the 29 autistic children, compared with none of the children in either of the comparison groups, showed abnormal endorphin fraction I levels (NS).

Endorphin fraction II levels   .

Fourteen of the 29 autistic children (48%) and none of the other children showed abnormal endorphin fraction II levels $(P<0.05$ IA/H, $P<0.01$ IA/(H + N)).

Endorphin fraction II levels in relation to
certain clinical characteristics of autism group

Tables I–III show the results of subdividing the autism cases into high and low fraction II endorphin levels (above/below comparison group H mean + 2 s.d.) according to self-destructiveness, sensitivity to pain and motor stereotypies. There is a clear indication that decreased pain sensitivity is associated with high endorphin fraction II levels in the autistic group.

Endorphin fraction II levels according to age, sex,
IQ, epilepsy and other associated handicaps

There were no clear-cut correlations between endorphin fraction II levels and sex of the child, intellectual level, or occurrence of epilepsy or of other

TABLE I
Self-destructiveness according to levels of endorphin fraction II in autism group

Autistic group levels of endorphin fraction II	Self-destructive	Not self-destructive
High	10/14 (71%)	4/14 (28%)
Low	6/15 (40%)	9/15 (60%)

Not statistically significant

TABLE II
Decreased sensitivity to pain according to levels of endorphin fraction II in autism group

Autistic group levels of endorphin fraction II	Decreased sensitivity to pain	Normal sensitivity to pain
High	12/14 (86%)	2/14 (14%)
Low	3/15 (20%)	12/15 (80%)

$P<0.01$

TABLE III
Motor stereotypies according to levels of endorphin fraction II in autism group

Autistic group levels of endorphin fraction II	High degree of current stereotypies	Low degree of current stereotypies
High	6/14 (43%)	8/14 (57%)
Low	3/15 (20%)	12/15 (80%)

Not statistically significant

associated handicaps. Age was not clearly associated either, but the mean age of the autistic children in the high endorphin fraction II group (7.9 ± 3.5, $n = 14$) tended to be somewhat higher than in the low endorphin fraction II group (6.3 ± 3.1, $n = 15$) (NS).

Repeat values

There was relatively good re-test stability with regard to CSF endorphin contents in the small group of four patients who were subjected to repeat lumbar punctures. Those with normal levels of endorphin fraction I and II had levels well within the normal range at repeat examination. Those with abnormal values on the first examination still had abnormal values on repeat analysis.

Discussion

This study represents an extension of the work in which we found autistic children to have high levels of endorphin fraction II in the cerebrospinal fluid (Gillberg *et al*, 1985). The results are in good accord with those of the previous study. It appears that levels of endorphin fraction II might be elevated in infantile autism. Abnormalities in the level of endogenous opioids have also been found in a study of blood from autistic patients (Weizman *et al*, 1984).

It is now almost ten years since Panksepp (1979) suggested that dysfunction of endogenous opioid systems of the central nervous system may represent the biochemical basis of certain behavioural symptoms and other kinds of problems seen in autistic children. Prior to that, Kalat (1978) had speculated on similarities between autism and opiate addiction.

In the analysis of our data we found reduced sensitivity to pain to be associated with high endorphin fraction II levels. Reduced pain sensitivity is common in autism. At the present stage it is impossible to sort out which is the 'primary' association: that between autism and opioid dysfunction or that between pain sensitivity and opioid regulation; or whether the finding as regards pain sensitivity and opioid activity is merely a reflection of the former being common in autism or vice versa.

There was a slight trend in our material indicating an association between endorphin fraction II levels and increasing age of the child. Obviously this factor has to be rigorously controlled for in future studies.

There is now a clear need for further studies of endogenous opioid functions in autism. Such studies should include mentally retarded children with and without autistic features and autistic children of normal intelligence. Further, it would be of great interest to study non-autistic children with reduced pain sensitivity. Correlational studies comparing CSF and blood samples for contents of endorphins are also warranted. To resolve the many outstanding issues in this field it is probably impossible — not least from the ethical point of view — to rely solely on CSF samples.

One clinical implication of our work is that opioid antagonists might be useful in the treatment of self-destructiveness — often associated with reduced pain sensitivity — in autism. To my knowledge, no good double-blind cross-over study of opioid antagonists versus placebo has been reported in the field of autism, but highly preliminary results from New York (Campbell *et al*, 1986) suggest that such studies might be a fruitful avenue for future research.

Acknowledgements

This study was supported by a grant from the Stallone Fund for Autism Research. I am grateful to the children and parents who participated in the study and to Lars Terenius and his staff for performing the endorphin analyses. Gun Jakobsson typed the manuscripts.

References

AMERICAN PSYCHIATRIC ASSCCIATION (1980) *Diagnostic and Statistical Manual of Mental Disorders*, (3rd edn) (DSM–III). Washington DC: APA.

CAMPBELL, M., SMALL, A. H., PERRY, R. & GREEN, W. H (1986) Pharmacotherapy in infantile autism: efficacy and safety. Elsevier Science Publishing Co. (eds C. Shagass *et al*).

COLEMAN, M. & GILLBERG, C. (1985) *The Biology of the Autistic Syndromes*. New York: Praeger.

DORES, R. B., AKIL, H. & WATSON, S. J. (1984) Strategies for studying opioid peptide regulation at the gene, measure and protein levels. *Peptides*, **5** (Suppl. 1), 9–17.

GILLBERG, C., TERENIUS, L. & LÖNNERHOLM, L. (1985) Endorphin activity in childhood psychosis: spinal fluid in 24 cases. *Archives of General Psychiatry*, **42**, 780–783.

HAGBERG, B. & RASMUSSEN, P. (1986) 'Forme fruste' of Rett syndrome — a case report. *American Journal of Medical Genetics*, **24**, 175–181.

KALAT, J. W. (1978) Speculations on similarities between autism and opiate addiction. *Journal of Autism and Childhood Schizophrenia*, **8**, 477–479.

PANKSEPP, J. (1979) A neurochemical theory of autism. *Trends in Neuroscience*, **2**, 174–177.

RUTTER, M. (1978) Diagnosis and definition. In *Autism: a Reappraisal of Concepts and Treatment* (eds M. Rutter & E. Schopler). New York: Plenum Publishing Corporation.

TERENIUS, L. & WAHLSTRÖM, J. (1975) Morphine-like ligand for opiate receptors in human CSF. *Life Sciences*, **16**, 1759–1764.

WEIZMAN, R., WEIZMAN, A., TYANO, S., SZEKELY, G., WEISSMAN, B. A. & SARNE, Y. (1984) Humoral-endorphin blood levels in autistic schizophrenic and healthy subjects. *Psychopharmacology*, **82**, 368.

YOUNG, J. G., KAVANAGH, M. E., ANDERSON, G. M., SHAYWITZ, B. A. & COHEN, D. J. (1982) Clinical neurochemistry of autism and associated disorders. *Journal of Autism and Developmental Disorders*, **12**, 147–165.

5 The role of genetics in the aetiology of autism, including findings on the links with the fragile-X syndrome

ANN LE COUTEUR

In this chapter I will consider the diagnosis of autism and the evidence for genetic factors, focusing separately on the genetic factors in cases where there is no known cause and a few genetic conditions for which an association with autism has been reported, such as the fragile-X chromosomal anomaly. I will then outline the family genetic studies that we are undertaking based at the Institute of Psychiatry.

Autism, a pervasive developmental disorder, is characterised by the presence of a particular pattern of behavioural characteristics that follow a particular developmental course, with some evidence of delay or deviance in the first 36 months of life (ICD–10 draft, World Health Organization, 1987). It seems clear that there is no single cause or aetiology to account for all cases of autism, although a single pathology or pathophysiology may perhaps be discovered to account for all cases. There is evidence (both from biological and epidemiological studies) which suggests that there are many aetiologies and that these described aetiologies are of organic origin. Among the cases for which an aetiology seems apparent, there are examples of physical, environmental (infections and perinatal trauma) and genetic causes.

Family and twin studies

Turning to the evidence for genetic factors in autism, and in particular to family and twin studies, the first question to answer is whether or not autism clusters in families. Excluding families with known or presumed genetic aetiologies, some familial aggregation of autism has been noted. In any interpretation of family data, and also of twin data, one must be aware of some of the hazards and factors that need to be considered when examining such data. Family and twin studies are prone to sampling biases, and unless sampling is systematic, certain families, for example those with several affected members, are much more likely to be reported than those with just one affected child. It is also necessary to consider the form that the diagnosis of the condition took—not only how the diagnosis was made and by whom—and whether the investigator who made the diagnosis knew that the individual he was assessing was a member of a family with another affected member. This may affect some of the judgements made about the individuals in that particular family. Finally, when the condition under investigation is defined by a set of clinical and behavioural criteria, it may be that to assume that the condition is inherited may falsely limit any investigation of familial aggregation. For these reasons it is important to include systematic measurements and a comparison group of families with which to compare the collected data.

Family studies

Taking into account all these factors, there is evidence from a number of studies to indicate that genetic factors probably play a major role in autism (Folstein & Rutter, 1987; Smalley *et al*, 1988). The pooled frequency of autism in the siblings of autistic individuals is 2.7% (Smalley *et al*, 1988)—a rate that is over 50 times higher than the general population incidence, using the narrower definition of autism of 2–4/10 000 (Lotter, 1966), and more than 10 times the population incidence that is found taking a broader defintion of autistic-like syndromes as used by Wing & Gould (1979) and Steffenberg & Gillberg (1986).

These estimates of rates in siblings do, however, need further replications using more standardised methods of assessment. For example, with the exception of the study by August *et al* (1981), none of the investigators systematically examined secondary cases in the family in the same way as the original probands. So it might be that these are mentally retarded children, or perhaps mildly autistic children, who would not meet the same diagnostic criteria as those by which their proband autistic siblings were ascertained. August and his fellow workers examined all their secondary cases but did not state whether these diagnoses were made blind to the diagnosis of their original proband sibling. All familial cases in this study were mentally retarded, so perhaps it might be that it is not so much autism as mental retardation that is being inherited in these families. Does this family aggregation of autism indicate genetic involvement? Twin studies may provide one approach to looking at this question in more detail.

Twin studies

There have been a number of reports of individual pairs of twins (reviewed by Rutter (1967), Folstein & Rutter (1977), Ritvo *et al*, (1985a) and Smalley *et al* (1988)). Most of these reported pairs of twins have been concordant for autism.

As with the hazards and limitations of reported family studies, so there are a number of factors that need to be taken into account in assessing the reported results of any twin studies. Gottesman & Carey (1983) summarised some of the questions to be considered. How were the samples ascertained? How was the zygosity determined? What diagnostic criteria were used for assessment? It is important to know if the data has been pooled for same-sex and opposite-sex twin pairs, and if any sex differences in the frequency of a trait and any variation in the severity or age of onset of a condition have been taken into account when estimating any correlations between twins (Smith, 1974).

There is a large literature concerning the complex mix of psychological and biological features that differentiate identical and non-identical pairs. Some of these factors tend to exaggerate and others tend to underestimate the role of genetic factors (Vandenberg, 1976; Scarr-Salapatek, 1979).

The number of identical twin pairs reported as single case studies does far exceed the number of reported non-identical twin pairs. This indicates a reporting bias, since in the general population non-identical twin pairs are twice as common as identical twin pairs. It is also known that twin pairs concordant for a condition, such as autism, are more likely to be reported than twin pairs discordant for a particular condition. This means that the proportion of concordant pairs in any report of individual pairs is probably an overestimate.

So, for the purposes of assessing possible genetic influences, it is necessary to study total population samples of twins. The first such twin study was by Folstein & Rutter (1977). This was a study of British autistic twins who had been systematically ascertained through multiple sources in the United Kingdom. The authors specifically urged the reporting of non-identical as well as identical twin pairs when collecting their sample of twins, and, when contacting the multiple sources of referral, emphasis was placed on the fact that the authors were equally interested in discordant and concordant twin pairs. The final sample of 21 pairs of twins meeting the diagnostic criteria for infantile autism appeared to be reasonably complete within the school age range. In this study the zygosity of the twins was determined using multiple blood group analyses for all pairs who were not seen to be clearly non-identical by systematic inspection of physical features. The final diagnosis was made by an independent psychiatrist who did not know the zygosity nor the twin pair membership of the individual twins.

In this sample the concordance rates for autism were 36% in the identical pairs and 0% in the non-identical pairs. The concordance rate was not explained by complications of pregnancy, delivery or postnatal illness, and it was therefore concluded that autism could be inherited. However, when a broader diagnostic definition was used, including additional cognitive and learning difficulties, the concordance rates for the identical twin pairs rose to over 80% and for the non-identical twin pairs to 10%. These findings demonstrate the need for further family and twin studies able systematically to consider a range of diagnoses, including the core diagnosis of autism, but also designed to consider possible subclinical variants of autism and other behavioural and clinical markers of conditions that may be associated with autism.

More recently Ritvo *et al* (1985*a*) have reported on another large series of twins where one or both have the diagnosis of autism. These authors claim a concordance rate of 95.7% for identical twin pairs and 23.5% for non-identical twin pairs. Although this is a larger sample than the original British twin survey, it is important to note that the majority of the pairs of twins were ascertained through one referral source, namely responding to an advertisement in a newsletter of the National Society for Autistic Children in America. As I have already indicated, this represents a form of ascertainment bias; therefore, although all diagnoses were made in accordance with DSM–III (American Psychiatric Association, 1980), the study findings cannot be taken as truly representative. The problems with the ascertainment bias in this study are further confirmed by the marked excess of identical twin pairs in the sample. Indeed, as the sample includes same-sex and opposite-sex pairs, there should have been twice as many non-identical twins as identical twins (Mittler, 1971), but the sample is reported as having equal proportions of both.

In summary, all these studies indicate that genetic factors are likely to be important, but that the nature of the genetic defect and the form that this defect takes remains unknown. It should also be noted that these studies (twin and family) all took place before the discovery of the fragile-X chromosome anomaly, and therefore how far this family aggregation in siblings is related to the fragile-X chromosome anomaly remains unknown.

Other genetic disorders in family members

As we have seen, as well as the familial aggregation of autism, aggregation of other disorders also seems to be present within the families of autistic children: principally disorders of general intelligence, and reading and language difficulties. This was first reported by Bartak *et al*, (1975), when a family history of reading or language disabilities was found in at least one first-degree relative in 5 out of the 19 families studied. In these families, all the autistic probands had an IQ within the normal range. The Folstein & Rutter (1977) twin study also showed concordance rates for disorders of cognition and language considerably higher than the concordance rates for autism *per se*. The severity of these disorders, for example among the identical twin pairs, varied from rather mild (a non-autistic twin requiring additional help with early reading) to more moderate (a non-autistic child with moderate mental handicap who required special schooling). For these twins, the role of perinatal complications seemed to suggest that a genetic predisposition to a condition in combination with an environmental factor may have contributed to the presentation of autism. Among the twin pairs concordant for a broader cognitive deficit but discordant for autism, where there was evidence of significant perinatal problems, it was the autistic co-twin who seemed to have had the more abnormal birth history. It is difficult to assess how applicable these findings are to the general population, since twins in general are more prone than single births to birth injuries and so may exaggerate the role of obstetric complication, and the injuries reported in case series of non-twin autistic children have been relatively mild. However, it might be possible that a mild birth injury could have a greater impact in a child who is genetically already predisposed to abnormal language or cognitive development.

As for studies of other autistic children (not twins), August *et al* (1981) and Minton *et al* (1982) compared siblings of autistic probands with age-matched comparison groups (for example, the August *et al* study compared the sibs with the sibs of children with Down's syndrome). The studies do tend to show evidence of cognitive disabilities: 15% had a mixed array of cognitive and language difficulties. More recently, Baird & August (1985) have confirmed these earlier findings in another sample, but on this occasion did find one family where aggregation was accounted for by the fragile-X chromosome anomaly.

In recent years, family studies have aimed to assess other aspects of possible genetic heterogeneity involving other conditions which might be related to autism, such as other social and emotional difficulties. In the past such studies (Cantwell *et al*, 1978) have found no increased incidence in, for example, the rates of other forms of psychiatric disorder in the family of autistic probands. Currently some studies are attempting to focus on some more subtle difficulties in social and emotional functioning. In the follow-up study currently being undertaken by Folstein and her colleagues in Baltimore, USA, some of the children originally assessed by Kanner have been contacted again now that they are adults (Table I). The preliminary data on the prevalence of disorder in siblings of these original probands and a group collected from the Maryland Autistic Society suggests a prevalence of 3% for infantile autism and an increased risk for other cognitive disorders (Table II). These preliminary findings also suggest an increased risk of severe social dysfunction and isolation and treated emotional disorder. This data is based

TABLE I
Baltimore study: sample characteristics and age of probands (Piven et al, *1988)*

| | Sample characteristics[1] | | Age of probands: years | |
	Probands	Siblings	Mean	Range
Total	37	67	35.6	22–55
Kanner	18 (14M, 4F)	20 (9M, 11F)	42.0	25–55
MSAAC				
(Maryland Autistic Society)	19 (14M, 5F)	46 (21M, 25F)	30.0	22–52

[1] M = male, F = female.

TABLE II

Baltimore study: risk and prevalence of disorders in siblings of autistic probands (Piven et al, 1988)

Disorder	Prevalence
Autism	2/67 (3.0%)
Severe social dysfunction and isolation	3/67 (4.4%)
Cognitive disorder	11/67 (16%)
Schizophrenia	0/67 (0%)
Treated affective disorder	10/67 (15%)

on the first-degree relatives of the first 18 (14 male, 4 female) of the original Kanner children to be recontacted, and 19 (14 male, 5 female) Maryland autistic subjects. The final findings of this study will be eagerly awaited. Our preliminary findings in the follow-up of monozygotic twins discordant for autism but concordant when younger for a broader range of cognitive difficulties also show that they do continue to show a similar pattern into early adult life, but that, for some, social difficulties are rather more apparent now than when they were younger.

Segregation analysis

Another means of investigating the possible form of inheritance of autism is to study 'multiplex' families. These are families specifically chosen for investigation because there is more than one affected child (with autism) within the same nuclear family. Ritvo and his group (1985b) in America have been studying a number of these families in recent years. The families have all agreed to take part as volunteers in this research work in response to recruiting advertisements. With the data collected from these families and in collaboration with Spence *et al* (1985), an attempt was made at segregation analysis. This is the investigation of possible genetic mechanisms using mathematical analyses to test the consistency of the gathered case material. For the Ritvo group such an analysis has reported data consistent with an autosomal recessive mode of inheritance, and was said to be not consistent with other multifactorial models. Although these results are intriguing, they consider only autism and not a broader range of cognitive abnormalities. In addition, the authors do not explain the great excess of affected males and the male–male sibling pairs in their own sample. So, although this particular study does not at the present time seem to clarify what is inherited, the research strategy is potentially a very fruitful one. Morton & Kidd (1981) do, however, discuss the dangers, particularly in child psychiatric disorders, of spurious results because of the uncertainties regarding the phenotype expression of the disorder. In conjunction with the segregation analysis techniques, linkage study analysis techniques can also be used with these multiplex families.

Linkage analysis

The purpose of genetic linkage analysis is to investigate whether the familial patterning of a trait or disorder, such as autism, is linked with a marker that is known to be the product of a single genetic locus (i.e. the physical mapping of genes and specific DNA sequences). If a linkage between the disorder and the marker is found, this does not imply that the marker (such as a blood group pattern or a HLA antigen) is related to the cause of the disorder, but simply that the gene for the marker seems to be close in position (a near neighbour), on a particular chromosome, to the disorders under investigation.

Gusella and coworkers (1983), using these techniques, have identified a locus linked to the gene for Huntingdon's disease. This has meant that it is possible to identify individuals with a high probability of being homozygous for this autosomal dominant neurodegenerative disorder.

Spe ..e *et al* (1985) have used these techniques with families with multiple cases of autism. Their work suggests that families with only boys affected might be genetically separate from those where at least one girl has the disorder.

This type of work does assume that for the families under investigation there is a unique chromosomal location for some gene for autism.

With current molecular genetic research techniques and the facility of restricted-fragment-length-polymorphism studies for gene mapping, there is an enormous potential for the detailed assessment of many regions of individual chromosomes, and so for the assessment of possible linkages with autism.

Single-gene disorders associated with autism

So far we have discussed the evidence for genetic factors in the aetiology of autism when the cases of autism do not seem to be associated with any currently discernible aetiological factor. However, there are certainly some cases of infantile autism that may be associated with particular medical conditions and other known genetic aetiologies. The study of such cases of known association is a further method of investigating genetic factors. The most frequently discussed genetic aetiology, at the present time, is the association between autism and the fragile-X chromosome anomaly. But there are a number of other conditions that have been shown to be associated with autism, some of which are known to be single-gene disorders.

Reiss *et al* (1986) have recently reviewed the evidence supporting the link between autism and some of these other known genetic conditions. Although these conditions are in the main extremely rare and therefore only represent a tiny proportion of all cases of autism, they are important in that they may suggest clues about the aetiology of other 'idiopathic' cases of autism.

Just as with the twin and family genetic data, there are some difficulties in interpreting the significance of the reports associating autism with these rare disorders. Firstly, such reports are usually in terms of single case studies and therefore are seldom based on systematically collected samples. Secondly, many of the reports do not describe the autistic subjects in sufficient detail to enable one to establish whether or not they meet currently accepted diagnostic criteria. Lastly, these gene disorders cover a number of very diverse clinical conditions, and so there is no obvious common pathophysiological mechanism that might act as a common pathway in the development of autism.

Phenylketonuria

Historically, phenylketonuria (PKU) was the first genetic condition to be reported in association with autism. This is an inborn error in metabolism which is inherited as an autosomal recessive disorder (Folling, 1934), and it is usually, although not always, associated with mental retardation. In the UK all newborn babies are screened for PKU, and if the screening test is positive a special phenylalanine-free diet is instituted within the first few weeks of life. Prior to early treatment, however, a few clinical reports described behaviours in children that did suggest that, in addition to the mental retardation, these children were severely deviant. In over half the cases the children were described as unfriendly, often mute and having repetitive behaviours. Hackney *et al* (1968) studied 46 children with documented PKU and reported nine of these as autistic. This report and a number of other reports do imply a much greater association between PKU and autism than would be expected if these two disorders were not causally related.

Tuberous sclerosis and neurofibromatosis

A specific association between autism and tuberous sclerosis has also been described. This is a neurocutaneous disorder inherited as an autosomal dominant condition. Among patients with tuberous sclerosis, 70% are found to be mentally handicapped. Patients suffering with this condition are frequently reported to show autistic behaviour (Taft & Cohen, 1971; Lotter, 1974; Manshein, 1979; Hunt & Dennis, 1987). However, despite this reported association there have been no systematic behavioural studies of a population of patients with this condition.

Another neurocutaneous disorder, neurofibromatosis, also inherited as an autosomal dominant disorder, has recently been reported in association with autism. Among children with neurofibromatosis, 10–20% have some degree of mental handicap. Gillberg & Forsell (1984) reported two cases of autism and one case of childhood psychosis with autistic features associated with neurofibromatosis. These children were discovered from a total of

51 cases of childhood psychosis of unknown aetiology, one half of whom were said to be autistic. In this study the authors found the association of childhood psychoses and neurofibromatosis to be 120 times greater than the expected population incidence. It is perhaps a little surprising that this association had not been noted previously, but without systematic family histories and physical examinations on each case, the diagnosis could easily be missed.

All these various single-gene conditions support two rather different hypotheses regarding the aetiology of autism. Firstly, the clinical syndrome may represent a constellation of behavioural difficulties rather than one homogeneous disease entity. The particular genetic disorders described may be especially likely to cause a pattern of central nervous system damage that then results in the clinical manifestation of the autism.

A second, rather different, hypothesis, which could also be supported by the current state of research, might be that the clinical picture of autism represents one point on a continuum of psychological dysfunction. All the genetic conditions briefly summarised seem to give rise to a spectrum of cognitive, linguistic, perceptual and behavioural abnormalities in affected individuals. This spectrum of deficits may range from minimal to severe multiple handicapping conditions. This type of explanation would be very similar to that described by Folstein & Rutter (1977) at the time of their twin data study. However, more recently, Folstein & Rutter (1987) have suggested that the same data could be understood in terms of single-gene disorder with variable penetrance due to non-genetic factors.

Fragile-X

During the past 40 years, numerous reports have appeared in the literature describing families in which mental retardation has been transmitted in an X-linked manner. Martin & Bell (1943) reported the first such family pedigree, which included 11 mentally retarded male members within two generations. This syndrome can be confirmed cytogenetically by the occurrence of a 'fragile' site on the long arm of the X chromosome at position Xq27. Webb *et al* (1986*a,b*) evaluated schoolchildren in England and found a prevalence of fragile-X-positive mental retardation in 1 out of 1350 males and 1 out of 2033 females, giving a total prevalence to fragile-X of 1 per 1634 in the schoolchildren studied. If these estimates and a 3% prevalence of mental retardation in the general population are used, then the fragile-X syndrome may account for 10% of all mental retardation. This means that the fragile-X syndrome is second only to Down's syndrome among known aetiologies for mental retardation associated with cytogenetic abnormalities.

However, as further investigations and information are made available, the condition, its presentation and detection, and the understanding of the inheritance and genetic mechanisms involved become increasingly more complex. Until recently, this syndrome was thought to be inherited as an X-linked disorder, meaning that affected males pass on the chromosome to all their daughters and to none of their sons, and that female carriers pass on the chromosomal abnormality to half their daughters and half their sons, so that manifestations of the condition are seen mainly in males and in a proportion of females carrying the affected X chromosome. It has become clear, however, that from both the clinical and the cytogenetic aspect, the presentation of this condition can be extremely variable, and the inheritance does not now seem so straightforward. This is confirmed by the work of Bundey (1987), that has shown that about one half of index patients have a mentally retarded relative, and the remainder present as isolated cases. Other authors (Pembury *et al*, 1986) have proposed that the chromosomal mutation involved in this condition may occur in two or more stages. Such a hypothesis could explain why the syndrome is so common, with a frequency that is unique for a single-gene disorder.

Physical characteristics

It is now understood that males are more likely to exhibit the typical physical features of fragile-X than are females, and males are more likely to be severely mentally retarded. The commonly described physical findings (Bregman *et al*, 1987) are macro-orchidism, characteristic facies and connective tissue abnormalities. These individuals are said to have somewhat long faces and large ears, to be relatively hypotonic, and after puberty to have enlarged testicles. Other associated features (Bregman *et al*, 1987) are mental retardation (variable), language abnormalities, and behavioural and psychiatric disorders. Among females known to be positive for the fragile-X chromosomal anomaly, the facial features and other physical features are extremely variable and it is now thought that they cannot be employed to aid diagnosis.

Method of detection

Sunderland (1977) was the first to document the ability to demonstrate the fragile site on the X chromosome when cells, usually lymphocytes, are grown in a special culture medium deficient in both folic acid and thymidine. The expression of the fragile site can also be enhanced by a number of techniques such as the addition of trimethoprim (TMP) to the folic-acid-deficient medium. At present, there is no clear evidence of a relationship between the cytogenetic expression (i.e. the percentage of cells seen with a fragile X site) and the clinical or psychometric findings.

Association with mental retardation

There have been some reports (Daker *et al*, 1981; Webb *et al*, 1981) of intellectually and psychologically normal males who, on cytogenetic testing, demonstrate the presence of the fragile-X chromosome anomaly.

Conversely, there are some so-called fragile-X families with clinically normal men (so-called normal transmitting males) who transmit the syndrome but do not appear to have the fragile-X sites themselves.

Turner *et al* (1980) found that overall about 30% of female carriers show some degree of intellectual impairment, but the degree is usually less than in affected males. They report that nearly all mentally retarded females in known fragile-X families do show fragile sites, but, as with the males, there is not a strong correlation between the percentage of fragile sites and level of intelligence. Paul *et al* (1984), however, have shown an inverse correlation between the percentage of fragile sites on the active X chromosome and the IQ.

Obligate female carriers are those women who have had fragile-X-positive sons or brothers and therefore from their family histories should have the fragile-X chromosome anomaly themselves. Fryns (1986), in a study of 144 such obligate female carriers, showed that in more than 30% of these women, mental development was borderline to subnormal, and that these women also presented with some psychiatric disturbances. A partial expression of the physical characteristics was shown by 28% of these carriers (especially among the mentally handicapped women), but repeated chromosome screening remained negative in more than 50% of these subjects. This makes accurate genetic counselling of an individual female at risk extremely difficult, but it must be said that all the women with partial clinical expression were fragile-X-positive on screening. Finally, this author made a very interesting observation that among these women carrying the fragile X there was a high rate of fertility, calculated to be a fourfold increase in the rate of twinning.

So, to summarise, before we move on to look at the links between the fragile-X chromosomal anomaly and autism, it is relevant to note that although this condition is aetiologically important in relation to mental retardation, there is variability in both the physical manifestations of the disorder and the psychometric and possible psychological correlates of the disorder. There is also a great deal of controversy about the actual expression of this abnormality. From the family history data it would appear that both for males and females some known carriers do express the chromosomal abnormality and other known carriers do not.

Fragile-X and autism

There have been a number of reported associations between autism and the fragile-X syndrome in males. This association was first reported by Brown *et al* (1982), and further reports have followed (Gillberg, 1983; August & Lockhart, 1984). The percentage of autistic males, usually with mental retardation, is about 5–15%, with an overall rate of about 8% (Blomquist *et al*, 1985; Brown *et al*, 1986). However, it still remains unknown what proportion of the reported sibling recurrence risk for infantile autism can be attributed to the fragile-X syndrome.

Considering the role of fragile-X in females with autism, there are very few reported cases in the literature. Hagerman *et al* (1986) reported two women, both mentally retarded, one mildly and one severely, with cytogenetic evidence of the fragile-X chromosome. Both these women showed that their inactive X chromosome was preferentially the normal X chromosome. My own data has recently established the presence of the fragile X in one autistic female from the original twin series. Both this young woman and her non-autistic identical sister demonstrate the anomaly. Perhaps this points to an association with the cognitive abnormalities that aggregate with autism as well as with autism itself (Le Couteur *et al*, 1988).

Genetic counselling

With the current state of knowledge and now with the facility of prenatal diagnosis, genetic counselling is promising but also increasingly complex. At present, prenatal diagnosis is carried out on foetal blood and is only reliable in male foetuses (Webb *et al*, 1983). It is hoped that in the future the fragile-X chromosome will be identifiable in chorionic tissue taken at 8–10 weeks of gestation. The molecular biologists in their continuing attempts to locate the fragile-X mental retardation gene may facilitate another method of prenatal diagnosis. To date, the linkage of DNA markers to the fragile site has not been helpful in this work.

Current research

The fragile-X syndrome continues to be a very exciting and interesting area of research, with new findings regularly being reported in the literature.

Institute of Psychiatry studies

The work reviewed here has demonstrated important areas where further research is urgently needed into the role of genetics in the aetiology of autism. The autism group at the Institute of Psychiatry have a number of ongoing studies which we hope will help to answer some of these complex questions.

There is the genetic twin study, involving two distinct groups of twins — the 21 pairs and their families originally assessed by Folstein & Rutter (1977), and a new sample of twins systematically collected over the last few years. For both sets the twins are both the same sex and one or both suffers from infantile autism.

There is the family genetic study, in which the families of 110 autistic individuals (70 male and 40 female) are being compared with the families of 40 individuals with Down's syndrome. This family study data will be pooled with the jointly planned similar-sized Johns Hopkins data set collected by Dr Susan Folstein and her colleagues in Baltimore, USA. This pooled data will determine whether the familial loading for cognitive disorders and for autism applies when systematic standardised measured are employed. The analyses have been planned to determine other matters also: firstly, whether the extent of familial loading varies according to such features as sex, IQ, perinatal history, the development of epileptic seizures, patterns of symptomatology, and the presence of the fragile-X anomaly; secondly, which of the heterogeneous range of cognitive and social disabilities are specifically associated with autism; thirdly, the extent and nature of the genetic heterogeneity (through examination of pedigree patterns and separate assessment of cases associated with the fragile X); fourthly, whether there are any gene–environment interactions; and finally, as far as possible, which mode of inheritance best fits the familial patterns of inheritance.

In conjunction with this work, a smaller investigation is being undertaken with a group of 25 autistic children who were adopted before the diagnosis of autism was made. This current programme of genetic research will produce findings over the next few years and it is hoped that these findings will help clarify the role of genetic factors in the aetiology of autism.

References

AMERICAN JOURNAL OF MEDICAL GENETICS (1986) Editorial comment. *American Journal of Medical Genetics*, **23**, 6–10.

AMERICAN PSYCHIATRIC ASSOCIATION (1980) *Diagnostic and Statistical Manual of Mental Disorders* (3rd edn) (DSM-III). Washington DC: APA.

AUGUST, G. J., STEWARD, M. A. & TSAI, L. (1981) The incidence of cognitive disabilities in the siblings of autistic children. *British Journal of Psychiatry*, **138**, 416–422.

—— & LOCKHART, L. H. (1984) Familial autism and the fragile X chromosome. *Journal of Autism and Developmental Disorders*, **14**, 197–204.

BAIRD, T. D. & AUGUST, G. J. (1985) Familial heterogeneity in infantile autism. *Journal of Autism and Developmental Disorders*, **15**, 315–321.

BARTAK, L., RUTTER, M. & COX, A. (1975) A comparative study of infantile autism and specific developmental receptive language disorder: I. The children. *British Journal of Psychiatry*, **126**, 127–145.

BLOMQUIST, H. K., BOHMAN, M., EDVINSSON, S. O., GILLBERG, C., GUSTAVON, K. H., HOLMGREN, C. & WAHLSTROM, J. (1985) Frequency of the fragile X syndrome in infantile autism: a Swedish multicenter study. *Clinical Genetics*, **27**, 113–117.

BREGMAN, J. D., DYKENS, E., WATSON, M., ORT, S. I. & LECKMAN, J. F. (1987) Fragile X syndrome: variability of phenotypic expression. *Journal of the American Academy of Child and Adolescent Psychiatry*, **26**, 463–471.

BROWN, W. T., JENKINS, E. C., FRIEDMAN, E., BROOK, J., WISNIEWSKI, K., RAGUTH, U. S. & FRENCH, J. (1982) Autism is associated with the fragile-X syndrome. *Journal of Autism and Developmental Disorders*, **12**, 303–308.

——, ——, COHEN, I. L., FISCH, G. S., WOLF-SCHEIN, E. G., GROSS, A., WATERHOUSE, L., FEIN, D., MASON-BROTHERS, A., RITVO, E., RUTTENBERG, B. A., BENTLEY, W. & CASTELLS, S. (1986) Fragile X and autism: a multicenter survey. *American Journal of Medical Genetics*, **23**, 341–352.

BUNDEY, S. (1987) The fragile X syndrome. *Practitioner*, **231**, 910–914.

CANTWELL, D., BATES, L. & RUTTER, M. (1978) Family factors. In *Autism: a Reappraisal of Concepts and Treatment* (eds M. Rutter & E. Schopler). New York: Plenum Press.

DAKER, M. G., CHIDIAC, P., FEAR, C. N. & BERRY, A C. (1981) Fragile X in a normal male: a cautionary tale. *The Lancet*, *i*, 780.

FOLLING, A. (1934) Phenylpyruvic acid as a metabolic anomaly in connection with imbecility. *Zeitschrift für Physiologische Chemie*, **224**, 169–176.

FOLSTEIN, S. & RUTTER, M. (1977) Infantile autism: a genetic study of 21 twin pairs. *Journal of Child Psychology and Psychiatry*, **18**, 297–331.

—— & —— (1987) Autism: familial aggregation and genetic implications. In *Neurobiological Issues in Autism* (eds E. Schopler & G. Mesibov). New York: Plenum.

FRYNS, J. P. (1986) The female and the fragile X: a study of 144 obligate female carriers. *American Journal of Medical Genetics*, **23**, 157–169.

GILLBERG, C. (1983) Identical triplets with infantile autism and the fragile X syndrome. *British Journal of Psychiatry*, **143**, 256–260.

—— & FORSELL, C. (1984) Childhood psychosis and neurofibromatosis — more than a coincidence. *Journal of Autism and Developmental Disorders*, **14**, 1–9.

GOTTESMAN, I. I. & CAREY, G., (1983) Extracting meaning and direction from twin data. *Psychiatric Developments*, **1**, 35–50.

GUSELLA, J. F., WEXLER, N. S., CONNEALLY, P. M., NAYLOR, S. L., ANDERSON, M. A., TAUZI, R. E., WATKINS, P. C., OTTINA, K., WALLACE, M. R., SAKAGUCHI, A. Y., YOUNG, A. B., SHOULSON, I., BONILLA, E. & MARTIN, J. B. (1983) A polymorphic DNA marker genetically linked to Huntington's disease. *Nature*, **306**, 234–238.

HACKNEY, I. M., HANLEY, W. B., DAVIDSON, W. & LINDSAO, L. (1968) Phenylketonuria: mental development, behaviour and termination of the low phenylalanine diet. *Journal of Pediatrics*, **72**, 646–655.

HAGERMAN, R. J., CHUDLEY, A. E., KNOLL, J. H., JACKSON III, A. W., KEMPER, M. & AHMAD, R. (1986) Autism in fragile X females. *American Journal of Medical Genetics*, **23**, 375–380.

HUNT, A. & DENNIS, J. (1987) Psychiatric disorder among children with tuberous sclerosis. *Developmental Medicine and Child Neurology*, **29**, 190–198.

LE COUTEUR, A., RUTTER, M., SUMMERS, D. & BUTLER, L. (1988) Fragile X in female autistic twins. *Journal of Autism and Developmental Disorders* (in press).

LOTTER, V. (1966) Epidemiology of autistic conditions in young children: 1. Prevalence. *Social Psychiatry*, **1**, 124–137.

—— (1974) Factors related to outcome in autistic children. *Journal of Autism and Childhood Schizophrenia*, **4**, 263–277.

MANSHEIM, P. (1979). Tuberous sclerosis and autistic behaviour. *Journal of Clinical Psychiatry*, **40**, 92–98.

MARTIN, J. P. & BELL, J. (1943) A pedigree of mental defect showing sex-linkage. *Journal of Neurology & Psychiatry*, **6**, 154–157.

MINTON, J., CAMPBELL, M., GREEN, W., JENNINGS, S. & SAMIT, C. (1982) Cognitive assessment of siblings of autistic children. *Journal of the American Academy of Child Psychiatry*, **213**, 256–261.

MITTLER, P. (1971) *The Study of Twins*. Harmondsworth: Penguin.

MORTON, L. A. & KIDD, K. K. (1981) The effects of variable age-of-onset and diagnostic criteria on the estimates of linkage: an example using manic–depressive illness and color blindness. *Social Biology*, **27**, 1–10.

PAUL, J., FROSTER-ISKENIUS, U., MOJE, W. & SCHWINGER, E. (1984) Heterozygous female carriers of the marker X chromosome: IQ estimation and replication status of fra (X) (q). *Human Genetics*, **66**, 344–346.

PEMBURY, M. E., WINTER, R. M. & DAVIES, K. E. (1986) Fragile X mental retardation: current controversies. *TINS*, **9**, 58–62.

PIVEN, J., GAYLE, J., CHASE, G., FINK, E., LANDA, B., WZOREK, M. M. & FOLSTEIN, S. A. (1988) A family history study of neuropsychiatric disorders in the adult siblings of autistic individuals (in press).

REISS, A. L., FEINSTEIN, C. & ROSENBAUM, K. N. (1986) Autism and genetic disorders. *Schizophrenia Bulletin*, **12**, 724–738.

RITVO, E. R., FREEMAN, B. J., MASON-BROTHERS, A., MO, A. & RITVO, A. M. (1985a) Concordance for the syndrome of autism in 40 pairs of afflicted twins. *American Journal of Psychiatry*, **142**, 74–77.

——, SPENCE, M. A., FREEMAN, B. J., MASON-BROTHERS, A., MO, A. & MARAZITA, M. L. (1985*b*) Evidence for autosomal recessive inheritance in 46 families with multiple incidences of autism. *American Journal of Psychiatry*, **142**, 187–192.

RUTTER, M. (1967) Psychotic disorders in early childhood. In (eds A. Coppen & A. Walk), British Journal of Psychiatry special publication no. 1. Ashford, Kent: Headley Bros.

SCARR-SALAPATEK, S. (1979) Twin method: defence of a critical assumption. *Behavioural Genetics*, **9**, 527–542.

SMALLEY, S. L., ASARNOW, R. F. & SPENCE, M. A. (1988) Autism and genetics: a decade of research. *Archives of General Psychiatry* (in press).

SMITH, C. (1974) Concordance in twins: methods and interpretation. *American Journal of Human Genetics*, **26**, 454–466.

SPENCE, M. A., RITVO, E. R., MARAZITA, M. L., FUNDERBURK, S. J., SPARKES, R. S. & FREEMAN, B. J. (1985) Gene mapping studies with the syndrome of autism. *Behavioural Genetics*, **15**, 1–13.

STEFFENBERG, S. & GILLBERG, C. (1986) Autism and autistic-like conditions in Swedish rural and urban areas: a population study. *British Journal of Psychiatry*, **149**, 81–87.

SUNDERLAND, G. R. (1977) Fragile sites on human chromosomes: demonstration of their dependence on the type of tissue medium. *Science*, **197**, 265–266.

TAFT, L. T. & COHEN, H. J. (1971) Hypsarrhythmia and infantile autism: a clinical report. *Journal of Autism and Childhood Schizophrenia*, **1**, 327–336.

TURNER, G., BROOKWELL, R., DANIEL, A., SELIKOWITZ, M. & ZILIBOWITZ, M. (1980) Heterozygous expression of X-linked mental retardation and X-chromosome marker from fragile (X) (q27). *New England Journal of Medicine*, **303**, 662–664.

VANDENBERG, S. G. (1976) Twin studies. In *Human Behaviour Genetics* (ed. A. R. Kaplan). Springfield, Il: Charles C. Thomas.

WEBB, G. C., ROGERS, J. G., PITT, D. B., HALLIDAY, J. & THEOBALD, T. (1981) Transmission of fragile (X) (q27) site from a male. *The Lancet*, *ii*, 1231–1232.

WEBB, T., GOSDEN, C. M., RODECK, C. H., HAMILL, M. A. & EASON, P. E. (1983) Prenatal diagnosis of X-linked mental retardation with fragile-X using fetoscopy and fetal blood sampling. *Prenatal Diagnosis*, **3**, 131–137.

WEBB, T. P., BUNDEY, S., THAKE, A. & TODD, J. (1986*a*) The frequency of the fragile-X chromosome among schoolchildren in Coventry. *Journal of Medical Genetics*, **23**, 396–399.

——, ——, —— & —— (1986*b*) Population incidence and segregation relations in the Martin-Bell syndrome. *American Journal of Medical Genetics*, **23**, 573–580.

WING, L. & GOULD, J. (1979) Severe impairments of social interaction and associated abnormalities in children: epidemiology and classification. *Journal of Autism and Developmental Disorders*, **9**, 11–30.

WORLD HEALTH ORGANIZATION (1987) *ICD-10 1986, Draft of Chapter V, Categories F00–99; Mental, Behavioural and Developmental Disorders*. Geneva: WHO.

6 The role of serotonin in autism

JANICE A. KOHLER

Abnormal levels of neurotransmitters or their metabolites have been implicated in many neuropsychiatric disorders. Those which have been most extensively studied are the indoleamines, such as serotonin; the catecholamines, such as dopamine; and the opioid peptides. The role of serotonin remains one of the most important areas of current research. Serotonin imbalance has been implicated in childhood attentional deficit disorders, depression, anxiety states, eating disorders, violent behaviour, the chronic pain syndrome and other neuropsychiatric disorders.

Chemistry of serotonin

Serotonin is a naturally occurring, biologically active amine. The primary substrate, the amino acid tryptophan, is obtained from the diet. This is converted to 5 hydroxytryptophan, which is decarboxylated to 5 hydroxytryptamine (5HT) — serotonin. 5HT can then be oxidised by the enzyme monoamine oxidase, and eventually the metabolite 5 hydroxyindoleacetic acid (5HIAA) is excreted in the urine.

Serotonin is found in the gastrointestinal mucosa, in nervous tissue and in platelets, which are neuroectodermal derivatives. It has many actions in the body, affecting the circulation, respiration, renal function and smooth muscle, in addition to the nervous system. Since serotonin cannot cross the blood–brain barrier, brain cells must synthesise it themselves. In the central nervous system, serotonin-producing neurones are located in the midline raphe nuclei of the lower pons and medulla, and project fibres to many areas of the limbic system and also to other areas of the brain. Catecholamines occur in the same parts of the brain as serotonin, and it is difficult to distinguish the roles of serotoninergic and adrenergic neurones.

Drugs which block the secretion of noradrenalin and serotonin, such as reserpine, frequently cause depression. Decreased appetite and sex drive, together with insomnia, may occur. Conversely, many depressive patients can be treated effectively with drugs which increase neurotransmitters at nerve endings by blocking re-uptake, such as tricyclic antidepressants and monoamine oxidase inhibitors.

Serotonin levels in neuropsychiatric disorders

Alterations in serotonin and its metabolites have been identified in patients during depressive episodes. A low concentration of 5HIAA was found in the cerebrospinal fluid of patients with suicidal behaviour, for example (Traskman & Asperg, 1981). Studying central neurotransmitters directly in living patients is impractical and attention has focused on using blood platelets as a model for presynaptic nerve terminals. Platelets are known to accumulate, store and release biogenic amines, particularly serotonin (Pletscher, 1968). Virtually all the serotonin circulating in the blood is carried by the platelets, stored in their 'dense bodies'.

Abnormal blood levels of serotonin have been reported in several neurological and psychiatric disorders. They tend to be low in Down's syndrome and phenylketonuria, and raised in some children with mental retardation or autism. The consistently low levels in children with Down's syndrome present an interesting contrast to the raised levels in some autistic children, especially in view of their differing personality profiles. Children with Down's syndrome are usually friendly and sociable, in marked contrast to the aloof, socially non-responsive autistic patients.

Raised serotonin levels have consistently been found in about a third of autistic children tested in various series (Young *et al*, 1982). The mechanism is not entirely clear, but both platelet numbers and platelet monoamine oxidase activity appear to be normal (Cohen *et al*, 1977). If serotonin degradation is normal, then increased uptake of serotonin could be the cause of hyper-serotonaemia. There are conflicting reports in the literature, with some groups finding a clear increase in platelet serotonin uptake in autistic children (Katsui *et al*, 1986), and other groups showing no abnormality (Langer *et al*, 1981).

Whatever the mechanism for hyperserotonaemia, if raised levels were related to autistic symptoms then lowering them might induce symptomatic improvement. High levels of serotonin in four autistic boys were reduced by the administration of L-dopa, but no change in global symptoms was observed (Ritvo *et al*, 1971). These results were difficult to interpret, since L-dopa is a dopamine agonist and hence does not have an isolated effect on serotoninergic neurons.

Trials of fenfluramine in autism

Fenfluramine, a phenylethylamine derivative, is an anorectic agent which has been in regular use for many years in the treatment of obesity. Extensive pharmacological studies have shown that it lowers brain serotonin in animals (Clineschmidt *et al*, 1978) and results in lower levels of 5HIAA in the cerebrospinal fluid of patients receiving the drug (Schoulson & Chase, 1975). Biochemical data indicate that fenfluramine promotes a rapid release of serotonin and may also inhibit serotonin re-uptake (Garattini *et al*, 1975).

A pilot study in three autistic boys suggested that not only did fenfluramine lower blood serotonin, but that a concomitant improvement occurred clinically (Geller *et al*, 1982). A multicentre study was then set up to assess the effects of the drug on a larger number of patients. The trial had the same basic structure in each centre. Subjects were given placebo for an initial four-week period, followed by fenfluramine at 1.5 mg/kg/day for four months, and finally placebo for a further two months. All subjects and investigators participating in data collection were blind to the code. Blood serotonin level and several tests of IQ and behaviour were performed regularly. A serial observation scale specifically for use with autistic subjects was developed (Freeman *et al*, 1986). This consists of 47 types of behaviour grouped into five categories: motor, affect, language, sensory and social. Students can be trained to code behaviour types on a four-point scale during defined periods of observation of each subject.

Results from three individual participant groups have been published (Ritvo *et al*, 1983; August *et al*, 1984; Kylkylo *et al*, 1985). Fenfluramine appears to be generally well tolerated, although some subjects became drowsy and lethargic initially. Reversible weight loss was recorded, rarely necessitating a change in medication. Blood serotonin levels in all patients consistently fell to between 50% and 60% of baseline levels, and rebounded following cessation of therapy

Ritvo *et al* (1983) reported some symptomatic improvement in their group of 14 patients. During the treatment phase, abnormal motor behaviour decreased as rated by the Ritvo–Freeman scale, and the Alpern–Boll developmental profile showed improvement on the self-help, communication and social scales. Behaviour deteriorated on return to placebo. In a further study the same patients were treated for eight months, and on some scales further gains were seen (Ritvo *et al*, 1984). August *et al* (1984) reported a significant reduction in behavioural symptoms in seven of nine children treated with fenfluramine, but Kylkylo (1985) observed clinical improvement in only two of ten patients treated. The latter group comprised mainly globally low-functioning children, and it was concluded that fenfluramine might be less effective in such subjects.

Combined data from 81 patients from nine separate centres in the multicentre trial (including the three groups reported on above) have recently been published (Ritvo *et al*, 1986) The largest centre contributed 16 patients, the smallest only three. These data seem to confirm that fenfluramine produces significant symptomatic improvement on both professionally administered and parent-reported scales. Overall 33% of the subjects were rated strong responders, 52% moderate responders and 15% non-responders.

The distribution of strong responders among the nine centres varied from 0 to 77%, which requires further elucidation, although, with such small numbers at each centre, interpretation of all the results must be cautious. The main criticism of this trial is that the placebo–drug–placebo design does not allow for assessing treatment order effect. In early double-blind cross-over trials of fenfluramine in obese patients, treatment order proved important (Duncan *et al*, 1965). This effect becomes particularly significant if the study population does not manifest stable behaviour over a period of time. A second experiment utilising a design which mitigates treatment order effects has therefore been commenced, involving an additional 99 patients at 14 medical centres.

There are two recent reports of trials of fenfluramine using a double-blind, placebo–drug cross-over protocol, with subjects being assigned randomly to initial drug or placebo group. Ho *et al* (1986) studied seven autistic boys and found no consistent or uniform improvement of behaviour or cognitive ability as measured by conventional psychometric assessment. Slight improvement in attention in high-functioning autistic children was seen. Kohler *et al* (1987) studied 20 autistic subjects and found no significant difference in the scores for autistic symptoms between those on placebo and those on fenfluramine. The mean scores at each assessment decreased throughout the trial, however, irrespective of the timing of fenfluramine administration, illustrating the effect of intervention. Six children were thought to be clearly better during one half of the trial by both parents and teachers, but of these six, two children were on placebo at that time.

In all the trials reported above the diagnosis of autism was made using DSM–III (American Psychiatric Association, 1980) criteria.

Toxicity of fenfluramine

Campbell *et al* (1986) studied the effect of varying doses of fenfluramine on ten autistic children in a hospital. The optimal dose was in the range 1.1–1.8 mg/kg/day, with a mean of 1.4 mg/kg/day. Marked irritability was seen on higher doses (1.38–3.63 mg/kg/day). In two patients the global improvement and in three the decrease of aggression or hyperactivity was only transient.

Although isolated reports of long-term neuronal toxicity in various mammals have been published, at present no data support long-term toxicity in humans at clinical dosages. In a review of 3000 patients, drowsiness, lethargy and fatigue were found to be the commonest side-effects, with a 7% incidence of irritability (Pinder *et al*, 1975). All these symptoms were quickly reversible. Continuous treatment for up to two years has been given, with no other side-effects. These data refer to adult patients, since fenfluramine has rarely been used in childhood, and detailed follow-up of children involved in long-term trials is mandatory.

Conclusion

Dr Ritvo and his colleagues are convinced that fenfluramine is a safe and effective treatment for some autistic patients (Ritvo *et al*, 1986). Opponents are equally vociferous and insist that the long-term efficacy of fenfluramine as a specific treatment for autism is open to question and that its effect in lowering blood serotonin levels is irrelevant to whatever therapeutic effect it may have (Gualtieri, 1986). Fenfluramine remains an experimental drug for the treatment of autism in children, and its use outside appropriately designed and carefully monitored clinical trials cannot be advocated.

References

AMERICAN PSYCHIATRIC ASSOCIATION (1980) *Diagnostic and Statistical Manual of Mental Disorders* (3rd edn) (DSM–III). Washington, DC: APA.

AUGUST, G. J., RAZ, N., PAPANICOLAOU, A. C., BAIRD, T. D., HIRSH, S. L. & HSU, L. L. (1984) Fenfluramine treatment in infantile autism: neurochemical, electrophysiological and behavioural effects. *Journal of Nervous and Mental Disease*, **172**, 604–612.

CAMPBELL, M., PERRY, R. POLONSKY, B. B., DEUTSCH, S. I., PALIJ, M. & LUKASHOK, D. (1986) Brief report: an open study of fenfluramine in hospitalized young autistic children. *Journal of Autism and Developmental Disorders*, **16**, 495–505.

CLINESCHMIDT, B. V., ZACCHEI, A. G., TOTARO, J. A., FFLUEGER, A. B., McGUFFIN, J. C. & WISHONSKY, T. I. (1978) Fenfluramine and brain serotonin. *Annals of the New York Academy of Sciences*, **305**, 222–241.

COHEN, D. J., YOUNG, J. G. & ROTH, J. A. (1977) Platelet monoamine oxidase in early childhood autism. *Archives of General Psychiatry*, **34**, 539–547.

DUNCAN, E. H., HYDE, C. A., REGAN, N. A. & SWEETMAN, B. (1965) A preliminary trial of fenfluramine in general practice. *British Journal of Clinical Practice*, **19**, 451–452.

FREEMAN, B. J., RITVO, E. R., YOKOTA, A. & RITVO, A. (1986) A scale for rating symptoms of patients with the syndrome of autism in real life settings. *Journal of the American Academy of Child Psychiatry*, **25**, 130–135.

GARATTINI, S., BUCZKO, W., JORI A. *et al* (1975) The mechanism of action of fenfluramine. *Postgraduate Medical Journal*, **51** (Suppl.), 27–34.

GELLER, E., RITVO, E. R., FREEMAN, B. J. & YUWILER, A. (1982) Preliminary observations on the effect of fenfluramine on blood serotonin and symptoms in three autistic boys. *New England Journal of Medicine*, **307**, 165–169.

GUALTIERI, C. T. (1986) Fenfluramine and autism: careful reappraisal is in order. *Journal of Pediatrics*, **108**, 417–419.

HO, H. H., LOCKITCH, G., EAVES, L. & JACOBSON, B. (1986) Blood serotonin concentrations and fenfluramine therapy in autistic children. *Journal of Pediatrics*, **108**, 465–469.

KATSUI, T., OKUDA, M., USUDA, S. & KOIZUMI, T. (1986) Kinetics of ^{3}H-serotonin uptake by platelets in infantile autism and developmental language disorder (including five pairs of twins). *Journal of Autism and Developmental Disorders*, **16**, 69–76.

KLYKYLO, W. M., FELDIS, D., O'GRADY, D., ROSS, D. L. & HALLORAN, C. (1985) Brief report: Chemical effects of fenfluramine in ten autistic subjects. *Journal of Autism and Developmental Disorders*, **15**, 417–423.

KOHLER, J. A., SHORTLAND, G. & ROLLES, C. J. (1987) The effect of fenfluramine on autistic symptoms. *British Medical Journal*, **295**, 885.

LANGER, S. Z., MORET, C., RAISMAN, R., DUBOCOVICH, M. L., BRILEY, M. S. & SECHTER, D. (1981) High affinity binding of ^{3}H-imipramine in brain and platelets and its relevance to affective disorders. *Life Sciences*, **29**, 211–220.

PINDER, R. M., BZOGDEN, R., SAWYER, P., SPEIGHT, T. & AVERY, G. (1975) Fenfluramine: a review of its pharmacological properties and therapeutic efficacy in obesity. *Drugs*, **10**, 241–323.

PLETSCHER, A. (1968) Metabolism, transfer and storage of 5HT in blood platelets. *British Journal of Pharmacology and Chemotherapy*, **32**, 1–16.

RITVO, E. R., YUWILER, A., GELLER, E., KALES, A., RASHKIS, S., SHICOR, A., PLOTKIN, S., AXELROD, R. & HOWARD, C. (1971) Effects of L-dopa in autism. *Journal of Autism and Childhood Schizophrenia*, **1**, 190–205.

——, FREEMAN, B. J., GELLER, E. & YUWILER, A. (1983) Effects of fenfluramine on 14 outpatients with the syndrome of autism. *Journal of the American Academy of Child Psychiatry*, **22**, 549–558.

——, ——, YUWILER, A., GELLER, E., YOKOTA, A., SCHROTH, P. & NOVAK, P. (1984) Study of fenfluramine in out-patients with the syndrome of autism. *Journal of Pediatrics*, **105**, 823–828.

——, ——, —— et al (1986) Fenfluramine treatment of autism: UCLA collaborative study of 81 patients at nine medical centres. *Psychopharmacology Bulletin*, **22**, 133–140.

SHOULSON, I. & CHASE, T. N. (1975) Fenfluramine in man: hypophagia associated with diminished serotonin turnover. *Clinical Pharmacology and Therapeutics*, **17**, 616–621.

TRASKMAN, L. & ASPERG, M. (1981) Monoamine metabolites in C.S.F. and suicidal behaviour. *Archives of General Psychiatry*, **38**, 631–636.

YOUNG, J. G., KAVANAGH, M. E., ANDERSON, G. M., SCHAYWITZ, B. A. & COHEN, D. J. (1982) Clinical neurochemistry of autism and associated disorders. *Journal of Autism and Developmental Disorders*, **12**, 147–165.

7 Biological and behavioural effects of magnesium + vitamin B6, folates and fenfluramine in autistic children

C. BARTHÉLÉMY; B. GARREAU; N. BRUNEAU; J. MARTINEAU; J. JOUVE; S. ROUX; G. LELORD

The use of drug therapy in autistic children is neither standardised nor well accepted. However, the possible usefulness of pharmacotherapy in autistic patients should not be neglected and deserves further study.

In critical reviews of drug research and treatment with autistic children, Campbell and co-workers (Campbell *et al*, 1977, 1981; Campbell, 1978) showed that:

(a) a great variety of pharmacological agents have been tested, involving neuroleptics, hormones, vitamins etc.

(b) the clinical response to these drugs was often deceptive, and at best moderate

(c) improved research design and methodology were needed.

These last ten years in the Child Psychiatry Unit of Bretonneau Hospital in Tours, France, we have explored in a systematic fashion the effects and indications of several drugs with different actions: folic acid; fenfluramine; and vitamin B6 plus magnesium. The experiment designs and the results of these studies are presented here. The discussion will focus on the methodological issues relating to such investigations.

Population and method

Subjects

Since 1977, about 100 autistic children, ages ranging from 3 to 16 years, have been involved in the therapeutic studies. They were in-patients at the Child Psychiatry Unit of Centre Hospitalier Régional in Tours.

All children received a complete diagnostic appraisal, including medical, neurological, psychiatric and psychological evaluations. The diagnosis of autism was made on the basis of DSM–III criteria (American Psychiatric Association, 1980), by two staff psychiatrists. Intellectual functioning was determined. IQs ranged from profoundly to mildly retarded (mean IQ 50).

Medication protocols

Two main types of experimental protocol were used: double-blind cross-over trials (drug versus placebo), and open studies for the identification of responsive children and for the long-term follow-up.

All studies began with a pre-treatment period (2–4 weeks), during which baseline evaluations were made. They all ended with a post-treatment period (2–4 weeks).

Evaluation of therapeutic effects

The therapeutic effects were evaluated using clinical, biochemical and electrophysiological measurements.

The clinical changes were assessed using a behaviour rating scale — the Behaviour Summarised Evaluation (BSE; Lelord *et al*, 1981; Barthélémy, 1986) (Table I) — which supplies information on the actual clinical state of the child. The first ten items of the scale deal specifically with autistic symptoms, the last ten items with associated features.

Each item is rated on a five-point scale (0, never; 4, always).

The 20 item scores can be added together to give a global score. The ten-item subscores for autistic symptoms and associated features can also be considered separately.

When the protocols were terminated, the parents and the medical team were asked to report for each child their global impression of the effectiveness

TABLE I
Behaviour Summarised Evaluation (BSE) scale

I *Autistic withdrawal* 1 Eager to be alone 2 Ignores other people 3 Poor social interaction 4 Abnormal eye-contact	IV *Motor disorders* 11 Stereotyped sensori-motor activity 12 Restlessness, agitation 13 Strange facial expressions, posture and gait

II   *Impairment of verbal and non-verbal*
   communication
5 Makes no effort to communicate
   using voice and/or words
6 Lack of appropriate facial
   expressions and gestures
7 Stereotyped vocal utterance,
   echolalia
	V *Inadequate affective responses*
	14 Auto-aggressiveness
	15 Hetero-aggressiveness
	16 Minor signs of anxiety
	17 Mood difficulties
	
	VI *Instinctual disorders*
	18 Disturbance of feeding behaviour

III   *Bizarre responses to the environment*
8 Lack of initiative, poor
   spontaneous activity
9 Inappropriate relating to
   inanimate objects or to doll
10 Resistance to change and
   frustration
	VII *Attention, perception and intellectual*
	   function disorders
	19 Unstable attention; easily
	   distracted
	20 Bizarre responses to auditory
	   stimuli

of the treatment, and their opinion on the advisability of readministering the medication.

Biological measurements were performed before, during and after treatment. The clinical response to treatment was examined in relation to biochemical and electrophysiological changes.

(a) Modifications in the metabolism of two neurotransmitters (dopamine and serotonin) were evaluated by measuring the urinary levels of homovanillic acid (HVA) and serotonin (5HT).

(b) Changes in the 'cerebral electrical behaviour' were evaluated by measuring the brain responses to auditory stimuli (auditory evoked potentials (AEPs)).

Study I: folic acid

The use of folic acid was originally proposed by Lejeune and co-workers for the treatment of behaviourally disturbed and retarded patients with the fragile-X syndrome (Lejeune, 1981; Lejeune *et al*, 1981).

The aim of the present study was to examine the clinical response to folic acid in autistic children and to determine if there was any relationship between behavioural improvement and positive results in the fragile-X test. (The results of this study have been reported by Barthélémy *et al* (1987).)

Subjects

Eighteen children (13 boys, 5 girls), aged from 3 years 6 months to 12 years 6 months (mean age 7 years 10 months) participated in the study. Diagnoses were made on the basis of DSM–III criteria (American Psychiatric Association, 1980). IQs ranged from mildly to profoundly retarded (mean IQ 50). The chromosomal study for fragile X was performed in all patients.

Medication protocol

All patients began with a two-week pre-treatment period (ANTE), during which baseline evaluations were made. Then they were given 0.5 mg/kg/day of folic acid for eight weeks. The study ended with a two-week post-treatment period (POST).

Evaluation of therapeutic effects

The effects of folic acid were evaluated using behavioural and biochemical measurements. The clinical effects were evaluated using the BSE.

Urinary homovanillic acid (u-HVA) assays were performed before, during (8 weeks), and after treatment according to the method detailed in Bruneau *et al* (1986) and Barthélémy *et al* (1988). Previous work reported that urinary

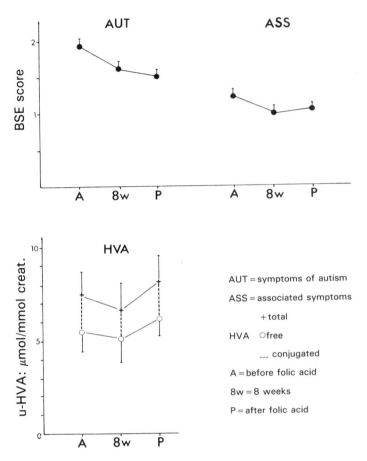

Fig. 1. Effects of folic acid on BSE scores and u-HVA (homovanillic acid) levels in eight responders

excretion of HVA was higher in autistic children than in controls (Lelord *et al*, 1978, 1981; Barthélémy *et al*, 1988; Muh *et al*, 1987).

Results

When all 18 patients were considered, decreases of both total and conjugated u-HVA levels were observed at the end of the eight-week treatment period, but behaviour did not improve for the group as a whole. However, according to the parents' reports, nurses' reports and BSE evaluation, eight children were clinically improved. In this subgroup of responders, the behavioural improvement was associated with a decrease of u-HVA levels (Fig. 1).

Two of the 18 children had positive results in the fragile-X test. Both of them were folic acid responders. Clear biochemical changes and behavioural improvement were shown by these two patients.

Study II: fenfluramine

Several studies have reported a notable improvement in certain clinical symptoms in autistic children after administration of fenfluramine. It was suggested that the positive behavioural effects of fenfluramine involved a serotoninergic mechanism (Geller *et al*, 1982; Ritvo *et al*, 1983; August *et al*, 1985). However, further studies showed that the clinical effects of fenfluramine could not always be related to its serotoninergic effects (Klykylo *et al*, 1985; Campbell *et al*, 1986; Ho *et al*, 1986; Stubbs *et al*, 1986; Ritvo *et al*, 1986; Barthélémy *et al*, 1987).

Results obtained from animal research showed that dopaminergic systems were also implicated in the pharmacological effects of fenfluramine (Garattini *et al*, 1975).

The aim of this study was to examine the effects of fenfluramine on both serotonin and dopamine metabolism in relation to the behavioural response to this treatment in autistic children. (The study has been reported by Barthélémy *et al* (1987).)

Subjects

Thirteen children (8 boys, 5 girls), aged 3–10 years (mean age 6 years 4 months), participated in the study. IQs ranged from 30 to 75 (mean IQ 50).

Medication protocol

A double-blind cross-over design, counterbalanced between patients for order of drug administration, was used. Patients were randomly assigned to the sequence fenfluramine–placebo (group 1, 7 subjects) or placebo–fenfluramine (group 2, 6 subjects). Investigators were not aware of which patients were in which group.

All patients began with a four-week pre-treatment period, during which baseline evaluations were made. The experimental phase then began, with group 1 receiving fenfluramine for 12 weeks followed by placebo for four weeks, and group 2 receiving placebo for four weeks followed by fenfluramine for 12 weeks. For all patients the trial ended with a four-week post-treatment period. In order to study after-effects of the drug, the different evaluations were also considered one month after the end of the treatment (i.e. at the end of the placebo period of group 1 and the post-treatment period of group 2).

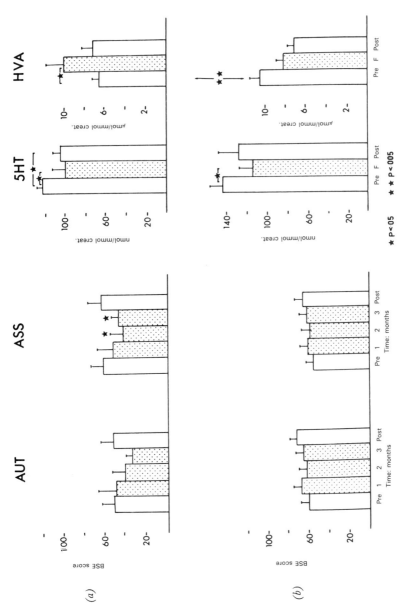

Fig. 2. Effects of fenfluramine (F) on BSE scores for autistic (AUT) and associated (ASS) symptoms, and on urinary levels of serotonin (5HT) and homovanillic acid (HVA) in the subgroups of (a) responders (n = 6) and (b) non-responders (n = 7). *P < 0.05; **P < 0.005

Medication was given in a twice-daily divided dose at a total dosage of 1.5 mg/kg/day. Dosages were reduced to 0.8 mg/kg/day in two children and to 1 mg/kg/day in two others since untoward effects emerged with initial dosages.

Evaluation of therapeutic effects

The clinical effects of the treatment were evaluated using the BSE scale. Each child was rated once a week during the whole study period. Scores were then averaged over periods of four successive weeks: five mean evaluations were obtained.

Parents' and nurses' reports were also considered.

Evaluations of urinary metabolites (serotonin (5HT) and HVA) were performed monthly as indicated in the protocol schedule. The serotonin assays were determined according to the method detailed by Jouve *et al* (1986). Only the values obtained after three months of treatment were used in the analysis.

Results

There was no significant overall effect of fenfluramine when considering the whole group of patients. However, a moderate decrease of mean urinary 5HT was observed in the third month of treatment.

According to parents' and nurses' reports and to BSE evaluations, six children were considered as responders. In the subgroup of responders, improvement was observed both for autistic and associated symptoms, but the improvement was significant only for associated features (Fig. 2).

A significant decrease in urinary 5HT was found in responders as well as in non-responders (Fig. 2). The main difference between groups concerned urinary HVA. The responders displayed a significant increase of HVA on fenfluramine treatment (from 6.6 ± 0.7, to 10.2 ± 1.8 in treatment, $P < 0.05$, Wilcoxon T test); whereas a slight non-significant decrease of HVA was observed in non-responders (Fig. 2). Moreover, the initial level of HVA differentiated the two groups, since it was significantly lower in responders (6.6 ± 0.7) than in non-responders (10.4 ± 0.9) ($P < 0.005$, Mann–Whitney U test) (Fig. 2).

Study III: vitamin B6 and magnesium

Vitamin B6 has been reported by several authors to give interesting results in some autistic patients (Heeley & Roberts, 1965; Rimland, 1974; Callaway, 1977; Rimland *et al*, 1978; Lelord *et al*, 1978, 1981; Ellman *et al*, 1981; Gualtieri *et al*, 1981; Barthélémy *et al*, 1981; Martineau *et al*, 1985, 1986). (The effects of vitamin B6 in Down's syndrome infants and in hyperkinetic children have been studied by Coleman (1979, 1985).)

Since 1977, several studies have been carried out in our department. The protocols of these studies were designed to examine the clinical response to vitamin B6 in autistic children and to determine the possible relationships between the behavioural results and biological data: urinary HVA levels and brain responses evoked by auditory stimulations (auditory evoked potentials (AEPs)).

Subjects and medication

The studies involved 91 children (56 boys, 35 girls), aged 2–16 (mean age 7 years 5 months). All selected children were autistic according to DSM–III criteria. IQs ranged from 20 to 70 (mean IQ 40). Medication was given at a total dosage of 25–30 mg/kg/day of pyridoxine chlorydrate and 10–15 mg/kg/day of magnesium lactate. Treatment duration varied from two weeks to eight months.

Experiment protocols

Four types of experiment protocol were used:
  (a) a short-term (two-week) open study (44 children) to identify B6-responsive subjects and to evaluate the behavioural B6 responsiveness
  (b) three short-term (two- or four-week) double-blind cross-over trials (61 children) to compare the clinical and biological effectiveness of vitamin B6 and magnesium either associated or given separately
  (c) a medium-term (two-month) open study on the biochemical, electrophysiological and clinical effects of a B6–Mg combination in 11 children already determined to be B6-responsive.
  (d) a long-term (eight-month) open study on the effects of combined B6–Mg in a four-year-old autistic boy.

Evaluation of therapeutic effects

The clinical effects of the treatment were evaluated using the BSE scale, each child being scored once a week during the whole study period. Parents' and nurses' reports were also considered. Urinary HVA levels were measured before and during treatment in all children. Brain potentials evoked by sensory stimulation (evoked potentials (EPs)) were recorded before and during treatment. A 'Pavlovian' paradigm coupling a sound with a light was used to 'sensitise' the auditory evoked potentials (AEPs), as detailed by Martineau *et al* (1986).

Results

From the initial group of 91 children, four subgroups could be determined according to the clinical response to B6–Mg treatment: 12 children were responders (14%), 30 children improved (33%), 39 children were unchanged (42%), and 10 children became worse (11%).

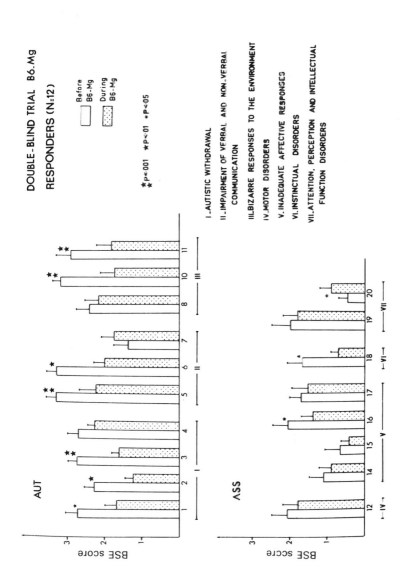

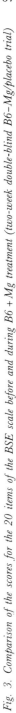

Fig. 3. Comparison of the scores for the 20 items of the BSE scale before and during B6 + Mg treatment (two-week double-blind B6–Mg/placebo trial)

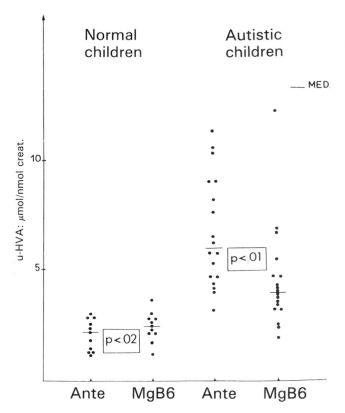

Fig. 4. Effects of B6–Mg treatment on urinary HVA level in autistic children (n = 18) compared with normal children (n = 11)

A careful analysis showed that, when compared with the unchanged children, the sensitive children were younger, and had a higher IQ, better language, and higher urinary HVA levels. They received smaller doses of B6–Mg combination and they received no or very little associated medication.

The behavioural changes observed in the improved children were significant for most of the first ten items of the BSE scale (i.e. the symptoms of autism) (Fig. 3). Simultaneously, the urinary levels, which were initially higher in autistic children than in controls, decreased after two weeks of B6–Mg treatment (Fig. 4). These behavioural and biochemical changes were associated with a tendency toward 'normalisation' of the conditioned AEPs (Fig. 5).

The combination of B6–Mg was much more effective than B6 or Mg given alone. The therapeutic effects were observed in the short-term as well as in the long-term trials.

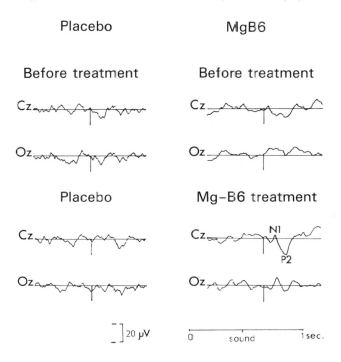

Fig. 5. *Effects of Mg–B6 treatment in conditioned AEPs in autistic children. The clinical improvement is associated with a tendency toward normalisation of the cortical response to sound (presence of wave N1–P2). (Cz = vertex; Oz = occipital).*

In the open medium-term study, 11 autistic children already found to be B6–Mg responders received B6–Mg treatment for eight weeks. A reduction of behavioural symptoms was observed after two weeks of treatment and was maintained over the rest of the eight-week course. The clinical improvement was accompanied by a decrease (for two weeks) followed by an increase (for eight weeks) of urinary HVA levels, and by an improvement in evoked potentials conditioning (after four weeks).

Discussion

Methodological issues

Type of patient

As infantile autism is rare, it is difficult to recruit for the same trial a sufficiently large and homogeneous group of patients. Among the various studies published, there probably exist notable differences concerning the purity and the stage of evolution of the autistic syndrome, the ages of the children, the intellectual levels of the children, etc.

Experiment design

A rigorous interpretation of the results calls for double-blind protocols. In cases of a cross-over, analysis of the results can be complicated: autistic children are subject to clinically spontaneous changes. A lag is frequently observed in the onset and ending of therapeutic effects. Effects are therefore wrongly attributed to the placebo. In any case, studies on long-term therapeutic effects are rare.

Evaluation criteria

Evaluation criteria must be measurable and reliable. The evaluation of therapeutic effects is based on the development and validation of scales. Some scales of this type have been elaborated (Lelord *et al*, 1981; Barthélémy, 1986). However, they are still insufficiently widespread at the international level. For this reason, it is difficult to compare clinical results obtained by different teams. It is necessary to add measurable biological parameters. This supposes the perfecting of exploratory techniques which are easy to apply and absolutely non-traumatic for the child, even if the examinations are repeated. Urinary assays are particularly useful for this reason.

Statistical analysis of the results

The samples of autistic children studied are generally small and the efficacy of the treatment is only moderate. The conditions for the application of statistical tests are difficult to satisfy. It is, however, possible to examine with precision the data concerning certain individuals, whether they are responders or not.

Discussion of results

Clinical and biological data obtained from our studies are in agreement with previous results. Indeed, in all three studies, when considering the groups of children as a whole, the clinical improvement was moderate at best. Since only some (but not many) children improved, we considered the possibility that the clinical changes occurred by chance.

To help evaluate this issue, we examined the relationship between the clinical changes and biological modifications under treatment in the subgroup of responders compared with non-responders. Simultaneous changes of behavioural and biological parameters were found in responders. However, we have to be cautious before linking the clinical response to any underlying mechanism through which the drug could be active.

For example, in the subgroup of folic acid responders, only two children showed a positive result in the fragile-X test. In the fenfluramine study, a subgroup of responder children could be evidenced, and the clinical effects in these children could not be related, as we expected, to fenfluramine serotoninergic effects, but instead to a probable drug action on dopamine metabolism.

The clinical improvement induced by the combination of B6 with magnesium was associated with improvement of 'cerebral electrical behaviour' and modification of urinary HVA: urinary HVA decreased at the beginning (two weeks) and then increased for medium-term and long-term treatment. Such differences between the acute and chronic effects of a drug on DA metabolism have already been described (Sedvall *et al*, 1974; Kendler & Davis, 1984). Again, the interpretation of such findings must be very cautious. However, our results lead us to point out the interest of such an innocuous medication for the treatment of some autistic children.

Conclusion

The rational application of new medications to autistic children depends on a better appreciation of the indications and a better evaluation of the therapeutic effects. Such progress, in turn, depends on the identification of clinical and biological markers specific to autism arising from investigations which must be, above all, easily applicable and non-traumatic for the child.

On the one hand such markers should be measuring tools, allowing a detailed and precise evaluation of the therapeutic effects; on the other, they could be used as predictive indices of sensitivity to different kinds of treatment.

Acknowledgements

This work was supported by INSERM 4316, Sécurité Sociale 1982 and Fondation Langlois.

The authors would like to express appreciation to Mrs. J. Chevreuil, A. Gabard, and the nursing staff of the Child Psychiatry Unit for participating in this research. They also thank Mrs M. Barre and H. Lehn for their technical assistance in the data analysis and the manuscript preparation.

References

AMERICAN PSYCHIATRIC ASSOCIATION (1980) *Diagnostic and Statistical Manual for Mental Disorders* (3rd edn) (DSM–III). Washington DC: APA.

AUGUST, G. J., RAZ, N. & DAVIS BAIRD, T. D. (1985) Effects of fenfluramine on behavioral, cognitive and affective disturbances in autistic children. *Journal of Autism and Developmental Disorders*, **15**, 97–107.

BARTHÉLÉMY, C. (1986) Evaluation clinique quantitative en pédopsychiatrie. *Neuropsychiatrie de l'enfance*, **34**, 63–91.

——, GARREAU, B., LEDDET, I., ERNOUF, D., MUH, J. P. & LELORD, G. (1981) Behavioral and biological effects of oral magnesium, vitamin B6 and combined magnesium–B6 administration in autistic children. *Magnesium Bulletin*, **3**, 150–153.

——, MARTINEAU, J., JOUVE, J., MORAINE, C., MUH, J. P. & LEJEUNE, J. (1987) Méthodologie d'études thérapeutiques contrôlées (vitamine B6, magnésium, halopéridol, folates, fenfluramine) chez l'enfant autistique. In *Autisme Infantile: Infantile Autism* (eds F. Gremy, S. Tomkiewicz, P. Ferrari & G. Lelord). *INSERM*, **146**, 265–272.

——, BRUNEAU, N., COTTET-EYMARD, J. M., JOUVE, J., GARREAU, B., LELORD, G., MUH, J. P. & PEYRIN, L. (1988) Urinary free and conjugated catecholamines and metabolites in autistic children. *Journal of Autism and Developmental Disorders* (in press).

BRUNEAU, N., BARTHÉLÉMY, C., JOUVE, J. & LELORD, G. (1986) Frontal auditory evoked potential augmenting–reducing and urinary homovanillic acid. *Neuropsychobiology*, **16**, 78–84.

CALLAWAY, E. (1977) Response of infantile autism to large doses of B6. *Psychopharmacology Bulletin*, **13**, 57–58.

CAMPBELL, M. (1978) Pharmacotherapy. In *Autism: A Reappraisal of Concepts and Treatment.* (eds M. Rutter & E. Schopler). New York: Plenum Publishing Corporation.

——, GELLER, B. & COHEN, I. L. (1977) Current status of drug research and treatment with autistic children. *Journal of Pediatric Psychology*, **2**, 153–161.

——, COHEN, I. L. & ANDERSON, L. T. (1981) Pharmacotherapy for autistic children: a summary of research. *Canadian Journal of Psychiatry*, **26**, 265–273.

——, DEUTSCH, S. I., PERRY, R., WOLSKY, B. B. & PALIJ, M. (1986) Short-term efficacy and safety of fenfluramine in hospitalised preschool-age autistic children: an open study. *Psychopharmacology Bulletin*, **22**, 141–147.

COLEMAN, M. C., STEINBERG, C., TIPPETT, J., BHAGAVAN, H. N., COURSIN, D. B., GROSS, M., LEWIS, C. & DEVEAU, L. (1979) A preliminary study of the effects of pyridoxine administration in a subgroup of hyperkinetic children: a double-blind cross-over comparison with methylphenidate. *Biological Psychiatry*, **14**, 741–751.

——, SOBEL, S., BHAGAVAN, H., COURSIN, D., MARQUARDT, M. & HUNT, C. (1985) A double blind study of vitamin B6 in Down's syndrome infants: Part I — Clinical and biochemical results. *Journal of Mental Deficiency Research*, **29**, 233–240.

ELLMAN, G., ZINGARELLI, M., SALFI, T. & MENDEL, B. (1981) Vitamin B6: its role in autism. Presented at the meeting of the National Society for Autistic Citizens, San Diego, CA.

GARATTINI, S., BUCZKO, W., JORI, A. & SAMANIN, R. (1975) The mechanism of action of fenfluramine. *Postgraduate Medical Journal*, **51**, (Suppl. 1), 27–35.

GELLER, E., RITVO, E. R., FREEMAN, B. J. & YUWILLER, A. (1982) Preliminary observations on the effect of fenfluramine on blood serotonin and symptoms in three autistics boys. *New England Journal of Medicine*, **307**, 165–169.

GUALTIERI, C. T., VAN BOURGONDIEN, M. E., HARTZ, C., SCHOPLER, E. & MARCUS, L. (1981) A pilot study of pyridoxine treatment in autistic children. Paper presented at American Psychiatric Association Meeting, New Orleans, LA.

HEELEY, A. F. & ROBERTS, G. E. (1965) Tryptophan metabolism in psychotic children: a preliminary report. *Developmental Medicine and Child Neurology*, **7**, 46–49.

HO, H. H., LOCKITCH, G., EAVES, L. & JACOBSON, B. (1986) Blood serotonin concentrations and fenfluramine therapy in autistic children. *Journal of Pediatrics*, **108**, 465–469.

JOUVE, J., MARTINEAU, J., MARIOTTE, N., BARTHÉLÉMY, C., MUH, J. P. & LELORD, G. (1986) Determination of urinary serotonin using liquid chromatography with electrochemical detection. *Journal of Chromatography*, **378**, 437–443.

KENDLER, K. S. & DAVIS, K. L. (1984) Acute and chronic effects of neuroleptic drugs on plasma and brain homovanillic acid in the rat. *Psychiatry Research*, **13**, 51.

KLYKYLO, W. M., FELDIS, D., O'GRADY, D., ROSS, D. L. & HALLORAN, C. (1985) Clinical effects of fenfluramine in ten autistic subjects. *Journal of Autism and Developmental Disorders*, **15**, 417–423.

LEJEUNE, J. (1981) Métabolisme des monocarbones et syndrome de l'X fragile. *Bulletin de l'Académie Nationale de Médicine*, **165**, 1197–1206.

——, MAUNOURY, C., RETHORE, M. D., PRIEUR, M. & RAOUL, O. (1981) Site fragile Xq 27 et métabolisme des monocarbones: diminution significative de la lacune chromosomique par traitement in vitro et in vivo. *Comyte Rendus de l'Académie des Sciences, Paris*, **292**, 491–493.

LELORD, G., CALLAWAY, E., MUH, J. P., ARLOT, J. C., SAUVAGE, D., GARREAU, B. & DOMENECH, J. (1978) L'acide hcmovanillique urinaire et ses modifications par ingestion de vitamine B6: exploration fonctionnelle dans l'autisme de l'enfant. *Revue Neurologique*, **134**, 797–801.

——, MUH, J. P., BARTHÉLÉMY, C., MARTINEAU, J., GARREAU, B. & CALLAWAY, E. (1981) Effects of pyridoxine and magnesium on autistic symptoms: initial observations. *Journal of Autism and Developmental Disorders*, **11**, 219–230.

MARTINEAU, J., BARTHÉLÉMY, C., GARREAU, B. & LELORD, G. (1985) Vitamin B6, magnesium and combined B6–Mg: therapeutic effects in childhood autism. *Biological Psychiatry*, **20**, 467–473.

——, & LELORD, G. (1986) Long-term effects of combined vitamin B6–magnesium administration in an autistic child. *Biological Psychiatry*, **21**, 511–518.

MUH, J. P., BARTHÉLÉMY, C., JOUVE, J., MARTINEAU, J., MARIOTTE, N. & BRUNEAU, N. (1987) Les monoamines urinaires dans l'autisme de l'enfant. In *Autisme Infantile: Infantile Autism* (eds F. Grémy, S. Tomkiewicz, P. Ferrari & G. Lelord). *Colloque INSERM*, **146**, 129–135.

RIMLAND, B. (1974) An orthomolecular study of psychotic children. *Orthomolecular Psychiatry*, **3**, 371–377.

——, CALLAWAY, E. & DREYFUS, P. (1978) The effects of high doses of vitamin B6 on autistic children: a double blind cross-over study. *American Journal of Psychiatry*, **135**, 472–475.

RITVO, E. R., FREEMAN, B. J., GEUER, E. & YUWILLER, A. (1983) Effects of fenfluramine on 14 out-patients with the syndrome of autism. *Journal of the American Academy of Child Psychiatry*, **22**, 549–558.

——, FREEMAN, B. J., YUWILLER, A., GELLER, A. *et al* (1986) Fenfluramine treatment of autism: UCLA collaborative study of 81 patients at nine medical centers. *Psychopharmacology*, **22**, 133–140.

SEDVALL, G., FYRO, B., NYBACK, H., WIESEL, F. A. & WODE-HELGODT, B. (1974) Mass fragmentometric determination of homovanillic acid in lumbar cerebrospinal fluid of schizophrenic patients during treatment with antipsychotic drugs. *Journal of Psychiatry Research*, **11**, 75–80.

STUBBS, E. G., BUDDEN, S. S., JACKSON, R. H., TERZAL, L. G. & RITVO, E. R. (1986) Effects of fenfluramine on eight out-patients with the syndrome of autism. *Developmental Medicine and Child Neurology*, **28** 229–235.

8 Urinary peptide metabolites in autism

FREDERICK J. ROWELL

Non-technical synopsis

A variety of components are present in urine, ranging from relatively large protein molecules down to simple salts. These components may be separated by liquid chromatography, a method in which the mixture is passed in solution through a column containing packing material for which the components have differing affinities. Components with low affinities for the packing material are washed or eluted from the column before those of high affinities, since the latter tend to 'stick' to the packing material and hence are delayed in their passage through the column.

The separated components which include proteins may be detected as they leave the column using light at a particular wavelength. It is therefore possible to obtain a graph of light absorption against the volume of solvent passed through the column. Under identical conditions of chromatography, samples having the same components will produce identical graphs or patterns of eluted peaks.

For the past decade workers in Scandinavia have described patterns obtained by chromatography of urine from patients suffering from a variety of psychiatric disturbances, including autism. Firstly, they precipitate proteins and protein-associated material from urine using benzoic acid dissolved in laboratory alcohol. After washing, the precipitate is dissolved and passed through the column. The elution pattern of the material is then monitored. These workers reported that there are three types of distinctive patterns associated with urine from autistic subjects which are different from urine of normal subjects. Further purification of the material obtained from the column using a second chromatographic column is also reported to produce distinctive patterns for autistics' urine. They also report a range of biological activities associated with the protein-like material eluted from the columns. The detailed nature of these active chemicals present in autistics' urine has not been published. It is argued that elevated levels of these urinary peptides (small proteins) is due to their elevation and/or reduced breakdown in autistic subjects, which results in their disruption of normal biochemical processes in the brains of such subjects.

We have not been able to reproduce the patterns obtained by the Scandinavian workers. However, we have demonstrated that a chemical is in the alcohol used in the Scandinavian laboratories which is absent from the corresponding type of British laboratory alcohol. This chemical must be present in order to achieve reproducible patterns using their method.

Using another method to extract material from urine, an American group have also reported differences in chromatographic patterns, between urine from normal subjects and from autistic subjects matched for age and gender. On further chromatographic purification of the material eluted from autistics' urine a component was isolated which has identical properties to a naturally occuring analgesic compound (met-erkephalin).

Replication of the above work by other workers could lead to its general use as a screen for the diagnosis of autism and to monitor its treatment. Further work is necessary to simplify present methods and to examine the links between autism and elevated levels of urinary proteins. This work would entail identifying these materials, establishing their origin and biological function, and determining the reasons for their changed levels in autism.

Introduction

Urine is a complex aqueous solution of common salts in which are dissolved a variety of small molecules, polypeptides and proteins. It is an ultrafiltrate of plasma and this filtration occurs in the glomerulus of the kidney. Only relatively small proteins pass into the urine from the blood in healthy individuals, with molecules of relative molecular mass greater than about 60 000 being excluded. The composition of the filtered liquid is subsequently modified in the distal tubule, where water reabsorption back into capillary blood may take place, and exchange of molecules into and from urine may occur by passive diffusion and active transportation.

Proteins may be separated from small solute molecules within urine by passing a small volume (0.1–0.5 ml) through chromatographic columns. These separate components according to the differing affinities of the urinary components for the material of the column (the packing or stationary phase). Components with a high affinity for the column material will tend to 'stick' to the column material, and hence their progress in a solution which passes through the column will be retarded compared with components which have lower affinities for the column material. Thus these lower-affinity components will leave the column before high-affinity ones as solvent is passed through the column. The affinity between components and column material may be due to charge–charge interactions between them, or may be due to differences in sizes in the components enabling molecules to penetrate into the porous interior of the column material to a greater or lesser extent. Thus

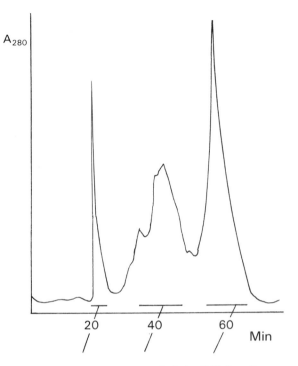

Fig. 1.   Gel chromatography of urine (0.5 ml) on Sephadex G-25 Superfine (Lindblom et al, 1983)

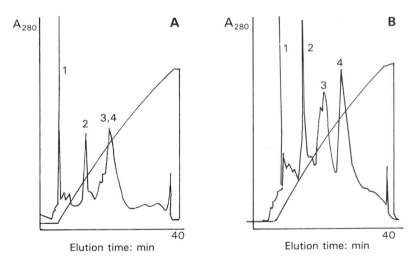

Fig. 2. Separation of urine proteins at pH 7.5 (A) and 8.5 (B) on a Mono Q column (Lindblom et al, 1983)

if large molecules do not enter the pores they will not be retarded, whereas small molecules which do will be retarded and hence will leave the column (be eluted) after the large ones.

An example of such size-exclusion — or gel permeation — chromatography occurs when urine is passed through a Sephadex G-25 column. The constituents separate according to size and are eluted. The presence of separated constituents in such elutes can be detected from the light-absorption properties of the molecules in solution. Fig. 1 shows a typical profile for urine passed through a Sephadex G-25 column. After about 20 minutes the proteins which absorb light at 280 nm are eluted, followed by a series of peaks due to ultraviolet-light-absorbing materials of lower molecular weights (Lindblom *et al*, 1983).

The individual proteins present in the protein-containing peak can be resolved using high-performance liquid chromatography (HPLC) or fast-protein liquid chromatography (FPLC), when columns having charged column packing are used, and eluting solvent is passed through the column under pressure to speed up the chromatographic processes. Fig. 2 shows peaks obtained from components absorbing at 280 nm and eluted from a Mono Q column (anion-exchange resin). Two traces are shown to illustrate changes in elution pattern which are observed using solvents of slightly different pH for the same sample. The major proteins observed are β_2-microglobulin (1), retinol-binding globulin (2), α_1-acid glycoprotein (3) and serum albumin (4). Of these, the latter two are the major constituents (Lindblom *et al*, 1983).

HPLC of the late-eluting peaks from the G-25 column through another anion-exchange column (Diaion CDR-10) resolves the low molecular weight

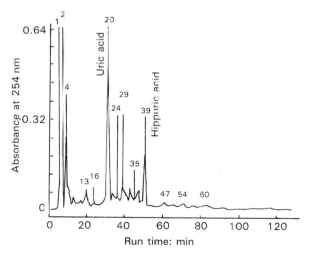

Fig. 3. *High-performance anion-exchange chromatogram of human urine on a Diaion CDR-10 column using perchlorate gradient elution (Seta et al, 1980)*

components into individual peaks. Fig. 3 shows an example of over 100 peaks, of which 33 have been identified. The major components showing strong absorption at 254 nm are uric acid (peak 20) and hippuric acid (peak 39). Of these, the former exhibits strong absorption at 280 nm (Seta *et al*, 1980).

Urinary elution profiles and disease

Proteinuria is a disease of the kidney which results in the excretion of proteins in excess of 100–200 mg/day due to increased permeability of the glomerular capillary membrane and/or diminished tubular readsorption. Different localisations of renal lesions are characterised by different molecular weight distributions of the urinary proteins. These result in differing patterns or profiles of elution peaks when urines are subjected to gel permeation chromatography. Patterns resulting from predominant excretion of proteins with lower molecular weight than albumin correlate with tubular damage, while those due to excretion of proteins of higher molecular weight are due to glomerular disease (Fig. 4; Ratge & Wisser, 1982).

Over the past decade, a group of Scandinavian workers has published a series of papers which suggest that specific patterns of urinary peptides and protein-associated peptides, detected by chromatographic analysis, are associated with a variety of psychotic disorders, including schizophrenia (Trygstad *et al*, 1980), anorexia nervosa (Trygstad *et al*, 1980), depression (Saelid *et al*, 1985), stress such as that associated with sleep deprivation (Trygstad *et al*, 1980), and childhood autism (Reichelt *et al*, 1981).

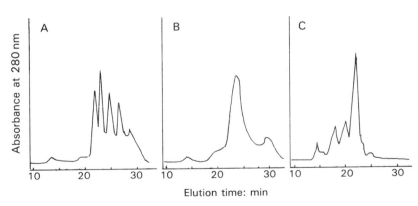

Fig. 4. High-performance anion-exchange chromatograms of human urine on TSK Cr 3000 SW columns: (Ratge & Wisser, 1982): (A) and (B) patterns obtained for renal tubular diseases, molecular weight (MW) 70 000–10 000; (C) pattern obtained for glomerular basal membrane disease, MW 600 000–60 000

The method of obtaining these urinary patterns is complex and slow. Its major steps are as follows.

(a) The proteins and protein-associated peptides are precipitated from large volumes of urine collected over 24-hour periods. This is effected by addition of 10% by volume of alcohol saturated with benzoic acid to the urine. The urine is shaken well and stood at 4°C for 18–20 hours.

(b) The precipated urine is centrifuged and the supernatant is discarded. The pellet is washed with alcohol by stirring and centrifuging until the absorbance at 280 nm in a 1 cm cell of the supernatant is approximately 0.4 OD units.

(c) The pellet is dissolved in ammonium bicarbonate solution, which, after centrifugation, is applied to a Sephadex G-25 (fine) column.

(d) The column is eluted at 36 ml/h with the ammonium bicarbonate solution (pH 8.50), and 1500 ml of eluate is collected in 10 ml fractions at 4°C. The eluate is monitored at 280 nm and the chromatograms are constructed.

(e) Fractions exhibiting material absorbing at 280 nm are evaporated and lyophilised overnight.

(f) The lyophilisate is suspended in acetic acid and centrifuged, and the supernatant is applied to a Bio-Rad P2 (fine) column.

(g) The column is eluted at 18 ml/h with 0.5 N acetic acid, 3 ml fractions being collected at ambient temperature.

(h) Aliquots from each fraction are dried overnight at 37°C, and then treated with potassium hydroxide at 100°C for 2 hours. To each is added hydrochloric acid, followed by potassium (or sodium) cyanide and ninhydrin. A blue colour develops, the intensity of which is monitored at 570 nm in 1 cm cells.

(i) Chromatograms are constructed to obtain a second elution pattern.

The above is essentially the original procedure that was described by Trygstad *et al* (1980) and Gillberg *et al* (1982). The patterns thus obtained for normal, schizophrenic and autistic subjects from G-25 columns are shown in Fig. 5. Some 25 autistic subjects were used in this study, diagnosed according to Rimland's criteria. All subjects had been without medication for at least four weeks prior to urine collection. Two distinct patterns were reported, described as types A and B. Of the 25 subjects (ages and genders not given), 2 had normal patterns, 2 had type II schizophrenic patterns, 13 had type A pattern, and 9 had type B. The retarded peak (900–1300 ml) was noted to contain relatively large amounts of uric acid derivatives in addition to some peptidic material. The material eluting at 600–900 ml when subjected to further purification (on Biogel P2) gave similar patterns for both type A and type B eluants. However, Reichelt *et al* (1986) noted that a corresponding analysis of the retarded material revealed considerable differences between the two types. Biological testing of the fractions from G-25 chromatography following a further 12-step purification process revealed activities similar to those obtained with corresponding fractions of urine from

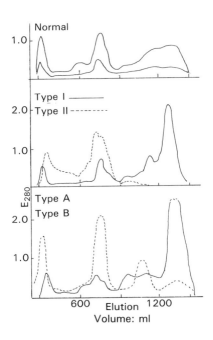

Fig. 5. Sephadex G-25 elution patterns following benzoic acid precipitation of urines from normal, type I and type II schizophrenic and type A and type B autistic subjects (Reichelt et al, 1981)

TABLE I

In vitro *activities isolated from the urine of autistic patients (Reichelt et al, 1981)*

Activity	Pattern type	G-25 elution volume: ml
Dopamine uptake inhibition	A	900–1300
Noradrenalin uptake stimulation	A & B	900–1300
Spiroperidol replacement	A & B	600–900
5HT replacement	A & B	600–900
Stimulation of 5HT uptake in platelets	A & B	600–900
GABA release	A & B	600–900
Glu release	A & B	600–900
QNB replacement	A & B	600–900

schizophrenic subjects (Table I). The authors reported that several of the peptides isolated from the urine of autistic subjects had been synthesised and were being checked for biological activity (Reichelt *et al*, 1981).

The following additional procedures are required to obtain the reported urinary profiles (Saelid *et al*, 1985; Reichelt *et al*, 1985; Reichelt, pers.

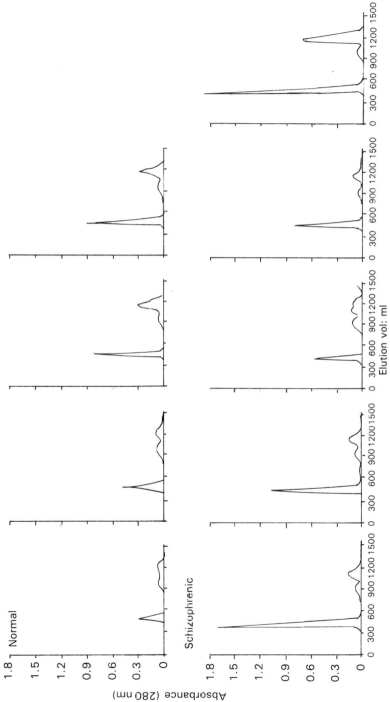

Fig. 6. Sephadex G-25 elution profiles of benzoic-acid-treated urine, with the region beyond 1500 ml elution volume deleted (Gilroy et al, 1988)

(i) In step (a), following addition of alcoholic benzoic acid solution, the pH of the precipitated urine is adjusted to between 4.0 and 4.3.

(ii) In step (b) the washing of the precipitate is selective, as only partial removal of the added benzoic acid is required.

(iii) Also in step (b), the washing alcohol contains 2% by volume of methyl isobutyl ketone (MIBK), this ketone being added to ethanol in Norway as an adulterant to deter people from drinking it.

We have demonstrated that without the presence of MIBK in the washing alcohol, the selective removal of benzoic acid in step (b) cannot be achieved (Gilroy *et al*, 1988).

Even with the modifications noted above, we have not been able to reproduce the G-25 elution profiles described by the Norwegian workers. Our patterns for normal and schizophrenic subjects are not significantly different, and are shown in Fig. 6. Likewise, we are unable to reproduce patterns reported for P2 gel chromatography. Those obtained by Reichelt *et al* (1986) are shown in Fig. 7, and our corresponding pattern in Fig. 8 (Gilroy *et al*, 1988).

In their most recent paper on autism, Reichelt *et al* (1986) suggest that the type B pattern obtained on G-25 chromatography can be subdivided into types B_1 and B_2. Type B_1 is associated with a large peak at 600–900 ml and two small peaks at 1100–1500 ml, whereas type B_2 is associated with only a large 600–900 ml peak, no late peak being present (Fig. 9). Details of the patients used in this study, the G-25 patterns obtained and the symptoms of the subjects are summarised in Table II.

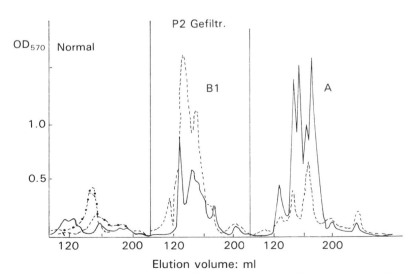

Fig. 7. Biogel P2 gel filtration patterns of the 600–900 ml peak from G-25 runs for normal subjects and types A and B autistic subjects (Reichelt et al, *1986)*

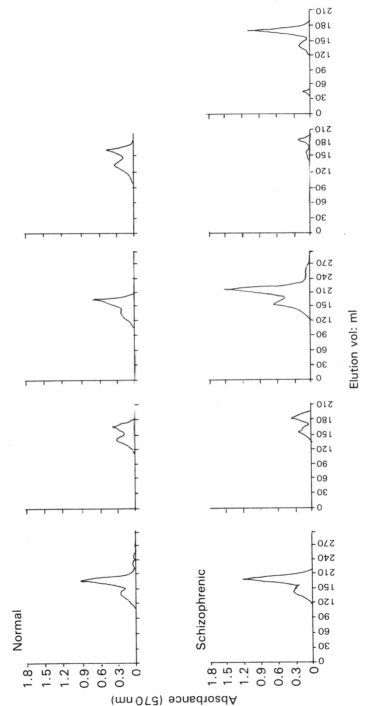

Fig. 8. Biogel P2 gel filtration patterns of the 800–1400 ml elution volumes from G-25 runs for normal and schizophrenic subjects (Gilroy et al, 1988)

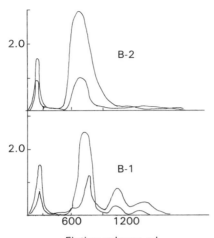

Elution volume: ml

Fig. 9. Sephadex G-25 gel filtration patterns of benzoic-acid-treated urine from autistic subjects (Reichelt et al, 1986)

TABLE II

Summary of urinary G-25 pattern types, subjects and their symptoms (Reichelt et al, 1986)

Urinary pattern type	Age (mean ± standard deviation)	Number	Comments/symptoms
A	7.2 ± 3.1	79	Not distinguishable from childhood schizophrenia pattern. Fulfilled all criteria for diagnosis of childhood-onset pervasive development disorder (DSM–III) except for that of onset before 30 months. Presence of a normal premorbid period and more aggressive and/or hypermotoric behaviour
B_1	6.4 ± 4.5	16	Fitted infantile autism criteria completely (DSM–III)
B_2	7.9 ± 5	50	Fitted infantile autism criteria completely (DSM–III). Only found in autistics living at home? Some B_2 patients can only be differentiated from normals by P2 chromatography.

The differences between our results and those of the Norwegian workers may be due to the presence of 20 % by volume of isopropanol in the ethanol used to prepare the benzoic acid solution in step (a) (Reichelt, pers. comm.). We are now re-examining G-25 urinary elution patterns from autistic subjects and normals in the light of this information.

Similar difficulties have been reported by Israngkun and his co-workers (1983) in replicating the results of the Norwegian group. This has led these workers to adopt an alternative method of isolating urinary protein and protein-associated material prior to G-25 chromatography (Israngkun *et al*, 1986).

(a) They lyophilise 24-hour urine samples and extract the resulting solid with acetic acid (4.5%, 2 ml/g of material) for 4 minutes and then add acetone (7 ml/g) and stir for 4 hours at 6°C.

(b) After centrifugation the acetone is removed from the supernatant by rotary evaporation and the remaining supernatant is centrifuged for 1 hour.

(c) The concentrated extract is applied to an Amberlite XAD-2 column, which is washed thoroughly with water and then eluted with methanol.

(d) The methanol eluate is treated with acetic acid (25 ml of a 1% v/v solution) and the solution is concentrated to 25 ml and centrifuged.

(e) The supernatant is applied to a Sephadex G-25 column, which is eluted with 1% acetic acid. Fractions (10 ml) are collected and the absorbance at 280 nm is monitored for these fractions.

(f) Fractions exhibiting absorbance peaks at 280 nm are pooled and lyophilised. Peptide material is detected as described in step (h) above for the previous method.

(g) Fractions containing peptide are dissolved in acetic acid and subjected to HPLC with a C-18 reverse-phase column, using 10% acetonitrile and 90% trifluoroacetic acid (TFA). The eluant is monitored at 215 nm. Samples (20 μl) are loaded and eluted over 16 minutes with an acetonitrile gradient (10–35%) in the TFA.

The G-25 patterns obtained by this method are shown for normal and autistic subjects in Fig. 10, and the HPLC patterns in Fig. 11. Israngkun *et al* report significantly different patterns in both types of chromatography for normal and autistic subjects. In this study there were 14 autistic subjects (11 males and 3 females aged 4–21 years) and 10 age- and gender-matched controls. The patients were diagnosed according to the Childhood Autism Rating Scale (CARS), and the DSM–III diagnostic category of pervasive developmental disorders. Only three of the autistic subjects had received medication in the six-month period prior to the study.

There were statistically significant differences in G-25 patterns between the groups. Peak II was higher in normal subjects ($P<0.01$), while the late peak, V, was higher in autistic subjects ($P<0.05$) (Fig. 10). The authors suggest that the presence of this latter peak is unique to autistic subjects and may be of diagnostic value. HPLC patterns obtained from fractions I and V were also different between the groups. A peak which co-chromatographed with met-enkephalin was observed only in fraction I from autistic subjects, and a peak with a retention time of 7.6 minutes was common

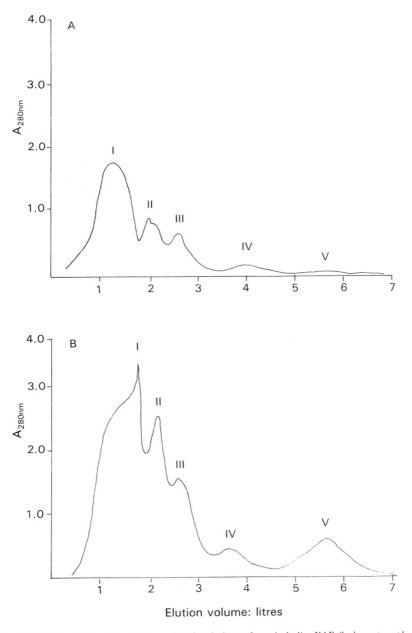

Fig. 10. *Sephadex G-25 elution patterns of methanol eluates from Amberlite XAD-2 chromatography of acetone/acetic acid extracts of urine from (A) controls and (B) autistic subjects (Israngkun* et al, *1986)*

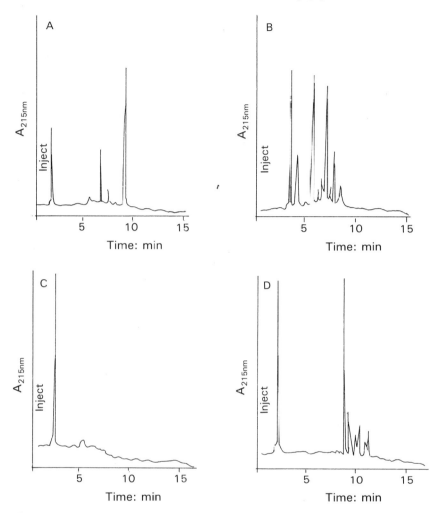

Fig. 11. Representative HPLC chromatographic patterns from fraction I of G-25 runs for the urine from (A) normal and (B) autistic subjects ana the corresponding patterns from fraction V for (C) normal and (D) autistic subjects (Israngkun et al, 1986)

to all autistic subjects but was absent from the corresponding peak in normal subjects (Fig. 11).

The nature of urinary peptides in autism

The major constituents present in the peaks obtained following Sephadex G-25 chromatography of urine from 11 autistic subjects have been determined (Reichelt *et al*, 1986). In common with schizophrenic subjects

TABLE III
Urinary protein in normal and autistic subjects (mean and standard deviation)

Subjects	Number	Age: years	Creatinine: g/l	Human serum albumin (HSA): μg/ml	α_1-acid glycoprotein (α_1-AGP): μg/ml	HSA/α_1-AGP
Normal	14	9.64 (3.1)	1.20 (0.54)	58.4 (80.8)	1.89 (1.65)	32.4 (32.0)
Autistic	15	9.40 (2.80)	0.98 (0.41)	23.7 (26.3)	1.27 (0.89)	19.8 (10.0)

(Reichelt *et al*, 1985), the peak at 600–900 ml contains lysozyme ($^{10}/_{11}$), α_1-acid glycoprotein ($^{11}/_{11}$) and albumin ($^6/_{11}$), but, in addition, IgG (γ-chain $^{11}/_{11}$ and F_c fragment $^9/_{11}$) molecules are present. Differences are also observed in the late-eluting peak (1100–1800 ml), since again IgG ($^{11}/_{11}$) is present together with lysozyme ($^{10}/_{11}$) in the peak from autistic subjects, while no IgG or lysozyme are observed in the peak from schizophrenic subjects. Other common proteins in this peak are α_1-acid glycoprotein ($^{11}/_{11}$) and albumin ($^6/_{11}$). Relatively large amounts of uric acid are also reported to be present in this retarded peak (Reichelt *et al*, 1981).

We have developed highly sensitive enzyme-linked immunosorbent assays for human serum albumin (HSA) and α_1-acid glycoprotein (α_1-AGP) (Phillips & Rowell, 1988) and used them to measure levels of these proteins in the urine of 14 normal and 15 age- and gender-matched autistic subjects. Samples were obtained first thing in the morning and stored at $-20°C$ until assayed. Creatinine levels were also determined and a multistix screen was performed. No significant differences between the groups were observed for creatinine, HSA, α_1-AGP or the ratio HSA/α_1-AGP, although creatinine and protein levels were higher for normal subjects (Table III). The multistix screens indicated that, for all subjects, blood was absent, urobilinogen normal, bilirubin absent, ketone absent, glucose absent, protein less than 0.3 g/l, pH 6.0–7.5, and specific gravity 1.000–1.030.

We have also demonstrated, using HPLC, immunoassay and other methods, that alcohol saturated with benzoic acid causes precipitation of both HSA and α_1-AGP from urine samples (unpublished results). It appears likely, therefore, that the enhanced absorption at 280 nm in the G-25 elution patterns of autistic urine samples is not due to elevated levels of these proteins.

In line with this conclusion are the results concerning the biological activities of urinary peptides eluted in the peaks from Biogel P2 columns. This gel separates compounds of relative molecular mass between 300 and 2000. The large proteins present in the peaks from the G-25 column are therefore eluted in the void volume on P2 columns, and the peaks observed are due to smaller polypeptides. As noted earlier, the Norwegian workers have further purified peaks from P2 columns and have ascribed biological activities to the purified materials (Reichelt *et al*, 1981). These materials have not yet been characterised, although they are described as consisting of amino-acids, one of which is usually an N-substituted N-terminal amino-acid with a clear-cut 205 nm absorption on HPLC analysis (Reichelt *et al*, 1986).

The American group have reported that HPLC of peak I from the urine of autistic subjects from G-25 chromatography shows the presence of a peak which co-chromatographs with met-enkephalin. This compound was also detected by radioimmunoassay (Israngkun *et al*, 1984). In a later paper, these workers state that the HPLC peak having the same retention time as met-enkephalin and found only in fraction V from G-25 chromatography in autistic subjects is not met-enkephalin since its molecular mass is different (Israngkun *et al*, 1986).

Conclusion

Replication of the results of the American and Scandinavian groups by other workers could lead to the use of the chromatographic patterns as screens for the diagnosis of autism and to monitor its treatment. However, further work is also necessary to simplify present methodologies — which take 2–3 days to perform per sample — and to examine links between elevated levels of urinary peptides and peptide-associated materials and autism. This will be achieved by characterising these materials, identifying their origin and physiological function, and determining the reasons for their changed levels in autism. Current speculation on reasons for the apparent increase in urinary peptide levels in autistic subjects include a reduced capacity to metabolically deactivate peptides — possibly due to reduce peptidase levels, or through their abnormal absorption, possibly in abnormally digested form, from the gastrointestinal tract (Reichelt *et al*, 1986). However, there is no current evidence to show that the putative peptides reported as increased in the urine of autistic subjects are found in the brain, nor evidence to suggest that abnormalities of peptidases occur in autistic subjects.

References

GILLBERG, C., TRYGSTAD, O. & FOSS, I. (1982) Childhood psychosis and urinary excretion of peptides and protein-associated peptide complexes. *Journal of Autism and Development Disorders*, **12**, 229–241.

GILROY, J. J., FERRIER, I. N., CROW, T. J. & ROWELL, F. J. (1988) Urinary chromatographic profiles in schizophrenia. *Biological Psychiatry*.

ISRANGKUN, P. P., PATEL, S. T., NEWMAN, H. A. I. & TAYLOR, W. A. (1983) Pattern of urinary putative neuropeptides in control and autistic subjects. *Clinical Chemistry*, **29**, 1287.

——, ——, —— & TEJWANI, G. A. (1984) Pattern of urinary putative neuropeptides in autistic and control subjects. *Federation Proceedings*, **45**, 1570.

——, NEWMAN, H. A. I. & PATEL, S. T. (1986) Potential biochemical markers for infantile autism. *Neurochemical Pathology*, **5**, 51–70.

LINDBLOM, H., AXIO-FREDRIKSSON, U.-B., COOPER, E. H. & TURNER, R. (1983) Separation of urine proteins on the anion-exchange resin Mono Q^{TM}. *Journal of Chromatography*, **273**, 107–116.

PHILLIPS, A. & ROWELL, F. J. (1988) A competitive enzyme-linked immunoassay for α_1-acid glycoprotein in serum and urine samples *Clinical Chemistry* (in press).

RATGE, D. & WISSER, H. (1982) Urinary protein profiling by high-performance gel permeation chromatography. *Journal of Chromatography*, **230**, 47–56.

REICHELT, K. L., HOLE, K., HAMBERGER, A., SAELID, G., EDMINSON, P. D., BRAESTRUP, C. B., LINGJAERDE, O., LEDAAL, P. & ORBECK, H. (1981) Biologically active peptide-containing fractions in schizophrenia and childhood autism. *Advances in Biochemical Psychopharmacology*, **28**, 627–643.

——, EDMINSON, P. D. & TOFT, K. G. (1985) Urinary peptides in schizophrenia and depression, *Stress Medicine*, **1**, 169–181.

——, SAELID, G., LINDBACK, T. & BOLER, J. B. (1986) Childhood autism: a complex disorder. *Biological Psychiatry*, **21**, 1279–1290.

SAELID, G., HAUG, J. O., HEIBERG, T. & REICHELT, K. L. (1985) Peptide-containing fractions in depression. *Biological Psychiatry*, **20**, 245–256.

SETA, K., WASHITAKE, M. & TANAKA, I. (1980) High-performance anion-exchange chromatography of human urine using perchlorate gradient elution systems. *Journal of Chromatography*, **221**, 215–225.

TRYGSTAD, O. E., REICHELT, K. L., FOSS, I., EDMINSON, P. D., SAELID, G., BREMER, J., HOLE, K., ORBECK, H., JOHANSEN, J. H., BOLER, J. B., TITLESTAD, K. & OPSTAD, P. K. (1980) Patterns of peptides and protein-associated-peptide complexes in psychiatric disorders. *British Journal of Psychiatry*, **136**, 59–72.

9 Does intrauterine cytomegalovirus plus autoantibodies contribute to autism?

E. GENE STUBBS

The cause(s) of the autistic syndrome remain unknown despite the findings of investigators that many disorders are associated with autism. Researchers generally agree that autism probably has many causes. The autistic syndrome may be a final common pathway resulting from metabolic disorders, infectious disorders, perinatal disorders, chromosomal disorders and structural disorders (Coleman & Gillberg, 1985). The final common pathway is likely to involve the limbic lobe and the cerebellum (Heath et al, 1980; Bauman & Kemper, 1985; Rivto et al, 1986). One promising, yet relatively unstudied, avenue of research is the viral–autoimmune study of autism. Chess and co-workers noted the association of autism and congenital rubella (Chess et al, 1971; Chess, 1977). We also noted the overlap in symptoms between children with autism and congenital rubella. Pursuing this possible cause and effect relationship, we found that autistic children, in contrast to control children, frequently did not have rubella antibodies, despite having a history of vaccination (Stubbs, 1976). This suggested that autistic children may have a relative anergy, or relative lack of response to the rubella antigen (virus). Thus, a clue that something was awry in the immune response of autistic children was suggested.

In addition to the association with the rubella virus, we also have found congenital cytomegalovirus (CMV) to be associated with autism in eight autistic children (Stubbs, 1978; Stubbs et al, 1984); Markowitz (1983) reported one case of autism associated with congenital CMV and a practitioner has personally communicated to me about another case, bringing the total to ten cases of autism associated with congenital CMV. We suspect that this is a gross underestimate of what the true relationship is between autism and congenital CMV. There are two reasons we believe this is an under-estimate. Firstly, most pregnant mothers never know that they have been infected. Either they have no symptoms or they may have a 'cold' or 'flu-like' symptoms; nothing is specific to CMV. Secondly, one out of 100 live-born babies shed virus in their urine, but most are asymptomatic. Only one out of 1000 are severe enough to have symptoms at birth, and so tests are run to make the diagnosis of congenital CMV. After the first week of life, one cannot make a diagnosis of congenital CMV with any certainty because post-natal infections are common from breast milk or from vaginal secretions and are usually benign. There are a significant number of children with congenital CMV who are asymptomatic at birth who will develop problems later, including learning disorders, mental retardation, deafness, hyperactivity and sociobehavioural disorders.

Most of the children that we diagnosed with a combined diagnosis of congenital CMV and autism had proven congenital CMV. However, in a few cases, the diagnosis was made in retrospect. We find that the younger the child is when one first sees and diagnoses autism, the more likely one will be able to culture CMV in the urine. Children who are severely affected with congenital CMV are likely to shed virus for years, sometimes up to 4–8 years of age. However, it should be emphasised that the presence of viral excretion or infection does not necessarily mean viral disease.

Recently, we cultured one autistic child whom we suspected of having CMV and found the child to be excreting CMV in the urine. We saw a second family, with identical twins, both of whom we diagnosed as having autism. This second family mentioned that the mother of the twins had contact during her pregnancy with the first mother and child, and also that the twins had a petechial rash at birth. We cultured the twins' urine for CMV and found them both to be excreting CMV. The mother of the twins had wondered if something was being transmitted from the first family to the second family. We know of a second set of mothers of autistic children who had contact during two of their pregnancies. However, the 'contact' pregnancies were not the ones that resulted in children later diagnosed to be autistic. The mothers did have some disturbances during their 'contact' pregnancies, however. One child was stillborn, and the other mother had a 'difficult' pregnancy and her child had multiple allergies. We have begun to take a pregnancy history of the siblings of autistic children as well as taking one on the autistic children themselves. We have found that even though the autistic child may have had a benign pregnancy and delivery history, the pregnancy histories of the siblings frequently are not benign. In fact, we have been intrigued by a relatively frequent finding of Down's syndrome siblings of autistic children. This also was noted by Coleman (1976) in her first book on autism. These observations led us to question whether autism may be a result of reactivation of latent CMV during the pregnancy, rather than a result of a primary congenital CMV infection. The primary infection with CMV would have occurred earlier, either during a previous pregnancy or at some previous time.

In addition to the viral association with autism, as mentioned above, we found some abnormal immune responses in autistic children. For example, autistic children had a decreased lymphoblastic response to the mitogen phytohemagglutinin (PHA), in contrast to normal control children (Stubbs *et al*, 1977). Warren *et al* (1985, 1986, 1987) also found a decreased lymphoblastic response to mitogens, including PHA, Pokeweed and Conconavalin A. Furthermore, they found a decreased number of T helper lymphocytes, a reversed ratio of T helper cells to T suppressor cells, and decreased cytotoxicity of natural killer cells in autism.

In addition to abnormal immunological findings, autoimmune phenomena have been found. Money *et al* (1971) reported the association between autism and autoimmune disease. He speculated that autoantibodies may be affecting the central nervous system. Sullivan (1975) noted an increase in an autoimmune disorder, rheumatoid arthritis, in families of autistic children, as did Raiten & Massaro (1986). We observed another autoimmune disorder, systemic lupus erythematosus (SLE), in a mother of an autistic child. Several other mothers of autistic children have a presumed diagnosis of SLE. Weizman *et al* (1982) found an abnormal cellular immune response to brain tissue in autism compared with other control groups. Todd & Ciaranello (1985) discovered antiserotonin autoantibodies to brain serotonin receptors in 30% of 30 autistic children, in contrast to groups of control children.

As mentioned above, SLE was found in one mother of an autistic child and presumed to be present in several other mothers of autistic children. Mothers with SLE have autoantibodies which can cross the placenta and affect the heart of the foetus, thus causing heart block. In addition, these autoantibodies can cross the mother's blood/brain barrier and cause neurological and psychiatric symptoms in the mother. We posed the research question: if these autoantibodies can cross both the placental barrier and blood/brain barrier, can they also affect the developing brain of the foetus and cause symptoms of autism? This research question led us to research findings on dyslexia; recently researchers in autism have discussed a continuum of autism and learning disabilities.

Behan *et al* (1985) found an increased incidence of antinuclear antibodies or autoantibodies, specifically anti-Ro antibodies, in mothers of dyslexic children in contrast to control subjects. They also reported evidence of brain dysplasia in the left hemisphere of dyslexic children. They postulated that transplacental antibodies may be contributing to dyslexia by affecting the development of the brain *in utero*. We decided to study autoantibodies in the autistic children and their mothers. This report is on our findings.

Method

Our initial experimental sample was 20 mothers of autistic children, with a control sample of 41 female Red Cross donors matched for age. At least one child of the experimental sample of mothers met the DSM–III criteria for infantile autism, and the diagnosis was agreed upon by a psychiatrist and a psychologist. We did not employ any exclusionary criteria in this preliminary study. Because of positive findings in the first study of mothers of autistic children, a second sample of 21 mothers plus 19 autistic children was studied. The control group consisted of 13 mothers and their 15 children, from the staff at the university and from the community at large. Mean ages and age ranges were as follows: for the mothers of the autistic children, mean 35 years, range 23–50; for the mothers of the normal children, mean 41 years, range 35–50; for the autistic children, 9 years, range 3–19; and for the normal children, mean 13 years, range 8–18. Thus, the experimental groups were slightly younger than the control groups. In the experimental group (autistic children), there were 15 males to 4 females, or about a 4:1 ratio, the usual ratio found in autism. In the control group of children, there were 9 males and 6 females, or about a 1½:1 ratio, with a smaller proportion of boys than the experimental group. Socioeconomic status (SES) was not matched between the two groups. The control group was probably of slightly higher SES status. Red Cross female donors, matched for age, served as a second control group for the study of antinuclear antibodies. The literature comparison group was derived from a large study performed by Duke University for standardisation of the assay. Results were taken from material sent with the assay from Immuno Concepts.

Antinuclear antibody screening of human sera was performed using the Indirect Fluorescent Antibody (IFA) test (Electronucleonics, Inc., Columbia, Maryland). Human epithelioid cells (HEp-2) were used as a second substrate for screening for antinuclear antibodies (Immuno Concepts, Sacramento, California). Rheumatoid factor was assayed using Latex Agglutination Test for Rheumatoid Factors (Rapi Tex RF Test, Behring Diagnostics, La Jolla, California). Thyroglobulin and microsomal autoantibodies were assayed by Haemagglutination kit (Wellcome Diagnostics, Dartford, England). We also studied circulating immune complexes by an enzyme-linked immunosorbent assay, Clq-IgG Elisa (Immunomedics, Newark, New Jersey). Cytomegalovirus Total Antibody Enzyme Immunoassay (Abbott) was used to assess CMV antibody.

Statistical methods used were Fisher's exact test of probabilities and chi-squared analysis to compare differences between experimental and control sample populations.

TABLE I

Frequency of positive antinuclear antibody test in mothers of autistic children and control groups

Antinuclear antibody	Mothers of autistic children	Mothers of normal children	Red Cross control women	Literature comparison group
HEp-2 substrate	7/41 (17%)	2/13 (15%)	4/41 (10%)	180/9000 (2%)**
KB substrate	9/41 (22%)	1/13 (8%)	9/41 (22%)	1/24 (4%)*
CMV antibody	12/20 (60%)	5/13 (38%)	—	—

* Significant at $P<0.05$
** Significant at $P<0.0001$

TABLE II

Frequencies of autoantibodies, cytomegalovirus antibody, and circulating immune complexes in autistic children and normal control children

Autoantibodies	Autistic children	Normal control children
Rheumatoid factor	0/19 (0%)	0/15 (0%)
Thyroglobulin autoantibody	4/19 (21%)	0/15 (0%)
Microsomal autoantibody	1/19 (5%)	0/15 (0%)
Antinuclear antibody (screen)		
HEp-2 substrate	4/19 (21%)	0/15 (0%)
KB substrate	5/19 (26%)	0/15 (0%)*
Combined antinuclear	6/19 (32%)	0/15 (0%)**
Combined total autoantibody	9/19 (47%)	0/15 (0%)****
Circulating immune complex	3/19 (16%)	1/15 (7%)
Cytomegalovirus antibody	4/19 (21%)	4/15 (27%)

	Girls	Boys
CMV antibody — autistic children	3/4 (75%)	1/15 (7%)***
CMV antibody — normal children	2/6 (33%)	2/9 (22%)

* Significant at $P = 0.04$
** Significant at $P = 0.019$
*** Significant at $P = 0.015$
**** Significant at $P = 0.0017$

Results

Results are shown in Tables I and II. There was a significant increase in antinuclear antibodies on both HEp-2 and KB substrates in mothers of autistic children when compared with the literature group, but not when compared with a local control group of mothers of normal control children or female Red Cross donors.

There were more CMV antibodies in the mothers of autistic children than in the control mothers, but the difference was not significant.

There was significantly higher antinuclear antibody with the KB substrate in the autistic children than in the normal children (Table II). There was also more antinuclear antibody with the HEp-2 substrate in the autistic children, but the difference did not reach significance. If the KB substrates and HEp-2 substrates are combined, the difference between the two groups increases, with the autistic children reaching 32%, compared with none in the normal children ($P = 0.019$). Thyroid antoantibody, although present in the autistic children and not present in the normal children, did not reach significance. When all autoantibodies are combined, including thyroglobulin and antinuclear antibody, the difference is very significant (47% versus 0%, $P = 0.0017$).

Neither the autistic children nor the normal children had any rheumatoid factor present. There was a slight increase in circulating immune complexes in the autistic children compared with the normal children, but the difference was not significant. There was not a significant difference in CMV antibody between the autistic children and the normal children. However, when one separates the children according to sex, there is a striking difference in the frequency of seropositive CMV antibody tests between the male autistic children and the female autistic children (1/15 (7%) males versus 3/4 (75%) females, $P = 0.015$). There were fewer autistic boys with CMV antibody positive tests than normal boys (1/15 (7%) versus 2/9 (22%)) but the difference was not significant. More autistic girls had positive CMV antibody tests than normal girls (3/4 (75%) versus 2/6 (33%)), but again the difference was not significant.

When one compares the number of positive tests with the number of negative tests, the autistic children have significantly more positive tests than the normal children (21 out of a possible 120 (17.5%) versus 5 out of 96 (5%), $P < 0.025$). When one looks at positive tests in the mothers correlating with positive tests in the children, excluding those cases which involve only CMV antibodies, the autistic children and their mothers have a significantly higher correlation (10 out of 19 (47%) versus 1 out of 13 (8%), $P = 0.019$). As for positive tests in the mother-child pairs, the autistic children and their mothers had significantly more positive tests between them (19 out of 19 (100%) versus 7 out of 13 (54%), $P = 0.0019$).

Discussion

The difference between autistic children and the normal control children in terms of total combined autoantibodies clearly differentiates the two groups, but not every autistic child demonstrated autoantibodies. However, there are a number of autoantibodies that have not been assayed in the two groups. The difference between the mothers of autistic children and local control mothers and female donors is not so clear-cut, but there is a clear difference when one considers controls from the literature. Although there was not a significant difference between the two groups of children for circulating immune complexes, there were more autistic children with circulating immune complexes. Also, the quantity of circulating immune complexes per child in the autistic children was much greater than in the one normal control child.

The frequency of CMV antibodies was not significantly different in the two groups of children, nor was it significantly different between the two sets of mothers. When one separates the sexes, there is a striking difference in the frequency of CMV antibodies between the autistic girls and the autistic boys (75% versus 7%, $P = 0.015$). The normal girls and boys have approximately the same frequency (33% for females versus 22% for males). The frequencies of the autoantibodies are approximately the same in the two sexes. This discrepancy of CMV antibodies may give one clue as to the 4:1 ratio of boys to girls in autism. Presuming that autistic boys and autistic girls are equally exposed to CMV, this finding suggests that boys are handling the CMV infection differently from girls. Males are known to be more·susceptible to infections than females. The CMV infection may do more damage in the male foetus, causing more cases of autism in boys.

However, in a genetically susceptible group, including both girls and boys, there may be a predisposition to develop autoantibodies in response to CMV which may contribute to brain dysfunction, and symptoms of autism. It may be that CMV contributes nothing to autism. However, it may be that both groups of children, autistic and normal, were equally exposed, but the autistic children may have been susceptible to developing the disorder. For example, their immune response to certain antigens may be low or their mothers may be low responders. CMV may be a necessary, but not sufficient, factor in bringing about autism in a subgroup of autistic children. The virus may set the stage, with the mother–child having an initial aberrant immune response (low response to the virus), or the mother–child may subsequently develop an abnormal immune response which in turn may develop autoantibodies. These autoantibodies may be operative through the mother, affecting the developing foetus, or may be operative within the autistic child; the child's own immune system may cause symptoms of autism by attacking his or her own brain.

Data derived from the mouse CMV indirectly support the viral–autoimmune hypothesis in autism. In the mouse, CMV can cause tissue damage, circulating immune complexes, and autoantibodies (Olding *et al*, 1976). If pregnant mice are infected, there are three outcomes: (a) a small percentage of mice die within four weeks after birth; all organs including the brain have inclusion bodies and viral antigen; (b) 25% survive and become chronic shedders of the virus; and (c) 75% survive and the virus becomes latent. In the latter two groups, neither the virus nor its antigen are found in any tissues, but can be co-cultivated out of the spleen. One strain of mice, C57Br/cdJ, in particular, despite 100% of the mice having been infected with the virus, manifests CMV antibody in only 60% of cases. This level of antibody is similar to that present in mothers of autistic children. As in human CMV, mouse CMV is capable of producing antinuclear antibodies, but only in the strain mentioned above, C57Br/cdJ. This strain of mice shows some interesting parallels with autism; that is, some autistic children have congenital CMV infections and antinuclear antibodies, just like the mouse strain C57Br/cdJ has congenital CMV infection and antinuclear antibodies; furthermore, the mothers of the mice have a similar percentage with CMV antibody as the mothers of autistic children. The mouse strain C57Br/cdJ is genetically susceptible to respond to CMV infection in a predisposed way. Likewise, autistic children and their mothers may be genetically susceptible to respond to CMV in a predisposed way including an autoimmune response.

The congenital rubella syndrome (CRS) also lends support to the viral–autoimmune hypothesis of autism. As mentioned above, the rubella virus has also been found to be associated with autism. In the CRS the virus can produce tissue damage (including the brain), circulating immune complexes, and autoantibodies (including autoantibodies to endocrine tissues). In studying CRS, investigators have come to recognise that some of the defects associated with this disease may appear months to years later (Sever *et al*, 1985). The authors have arbitrarily divided the CRS into three groups according to time of appearance: (a) newborn CRS, which includes damage that is apparent in the newborn period; (b) extended CRS, which includes damage that was present in the newborn period, but did not become apparent until late; and (c) delayed CRS, which includes new damage that was not present in early life. A similar delay in onset of defects may be applicable to congenital CMV and its possible relationship to autism. Congenital CMV is known to be capable of causing a delayed onset of deafness, especially within the first two years of life. With respect to delayed CRS, diabetes mellitus is the most frequent finding. It occurs in about 20% of patients with CRS in either an overt or a latent form by 35 years of age. The age of onset varies from 18 months to 33 years. Rubella virus has been isolated from pancreatic tissue of several infants who died of CRS, but there have been no reports of detection of rubella virus or antigens in the pancreatic tissue, or of elevated titres of rubella antibody of diabetic patients with CRS, both of which would be expected if diabetes mellitus developed as a consequence of viral persistence in the pancreatic tissues of these patients. Instead, the rubella virus may stimulate an autoimmune reaction which in turn would produce a gradual depletion of pancreatic islet cells after the virus was gone (Sever *et al*, 1985). This conceivably could happen in autism and congenital CMV as well. Instead of elevated CMV antibody levels with the virus or antigen being found in the brain, autoantibodies to peripheral tissues and to the brain could occur after the virus is gone or has become latent.

Thyroid disease, including hyperthyroidism, hypothyroidism, and thyroiditis, is another delayed manifestation of CRS. As mentioned above, thyroid autoantibodies were found in autistic children in contrast to none being found in normal control children. Thus, there are many similarities between CMV and rubella.

There are some important parallels between the abnormal immune findings in autism and the abnormal immune effects caused by CMV. CMV infections are immunosuppressive (Ho, 1984). The lymphoblastic response to mitogens like PHA is decreased in acute CMV infections in adults. There is also a decrease in T helper cells, with a reversal of the T helper/T suppressor cell ratio (Carney *et al*, 1981).

In pregnant women, Gehrz *et al* (1981) found that CMV-specific lymphoblastic proliferation response was decreased in normal uninfected seropositive mothers during the second and third trimesters, while responses to other antigens remained normal. This may indicate a peculiar inability of pregnant women to mount cellular immune responses to CMV at certain times during pregnancy (Ho, 1984). The specific CMV proliferative response is also depressed in infected pregnant women as well as in congenitally infected babies (Starr *et al*, 1979).

Most of the above-mentioned immune suppression phenomena have also been found in autism: namely, that autistic children tend to have a decreased lymphoblastic response to mitogens, and have a decrease in T helper cells, with a reversal of T helper/T suppressor cell ratio. In addition, they have a decreased natural killer cell cytotoxicity.

Circulating immune complexes, although not significantly different between the two groups, may be more important than the figures show. One may need to study younger children or be closer to the proposed time of the initial insult to capture the true incidence of circulating immune complexes. Circulating immune complexes are very likely to form in situations where there is an excess of antigen or of antibody. The hypothetical mechanism by which circulating immune complexes could contribute to autism is that the virus–antibody complexes could lodge in the choroid plexus which has Fc receptors, thus causing an inflammatory response which might directly interfere with brain function, or indirectly interfere by allowing the virus direct access to the surrounding brain tissue because the inflammation has opened up the blood/brain barrier. The choroid plexus surrounds the areas of the brain likely to be involved in autism, namely the limbic system and the cerebellum.

The hypothetical mechanism by which autoantibodies might contribute to the autistic syndrome could be either via maternal transplacental autoantibodies which could affect the developing brain of the foetus, or the autoantibodies might develop in the autistic child after birth and thus interfere with brain function of the autistic child. These mechanisms are not mutually exclusive; they could combine to contribute to symptoms. The mechanisms have the potential for causing a certain amount of irreparable damage, as well as contributing to ongoing, intermittent exacerbations of symptoms.

An integration of the above abnormal findings in autistic children might involve the following scenario. Firstly, there may be a genetic susceptibility to respond to viruses or other foreign antigens in an abnormal way, either through the mother or child or both. Secondly, the abnormal immune response could lead to production of destructive or disruptive autoantibodies by the mother and/or the autistic child. Also, circulating immune complexes could play a part. Finally, other intercurrent infections, stresses, foreign antigens, and/or hormones may contribute to episodic symptoms. Symptoms may abate or worsen depending upon the degree of exposure to insults versus the host's defences.

We recommend more research on the viral–autoimmune hypothesis of autism.

References

BAUMAN, M. L. & KEMPER, T. L. (1985) Histoanatomic observations of the brain in early infantile autism. *Neurology*, **35**, 866–874.

BEHAN, M. H., BEHAN, P. O. & GESCHWIND, N. (1985) Anti-Ro antibody in mothers of dyslexic children. *Developmental Medicine & Child Neurology*, **27**, 538–542.

CARNEY, W. P., RUBIN, R. H., HOFFMAN, R. A., HANSEN, W. P., HEALEY, K. & HIRSCH, M. S. (1981) Analysis of T lymphocyte subsets in cytomegalovirus mononucleosis. *Journal of Immunology*, **126**, 2114–2116.

CHESS, S. (1977) Follow-up report on autism in congenital rubella. *Journal of Autism and Developmental Disorders*, **7**, 69–81.

——, KORN, S. J. & FERNANDEZ, P. B. (1971) *Psychiatric Disorders of Children with Congenital Rubella*. New York: Brunner/Mazel.

COLEMAN, M. (1976) *The Autistic Syndromes*. New York: American Elsevier Publishing Company.

—— & GILLBERG, C. (1985) *The Biology of the Autistic Syndromes*. New York: Praeger Publishers.

GEHRZ, R. C., CHRISTIANSON, W. R., LINNER, K. M., CONROY, M. M., McCUE, S. A. & BALFOUR, H. H. Jr. (1981) Cytomegalovirus-specific humoral and cellular immune responses in human pregnancy. *Journal of Infectious Disease*, **143**, 391–395.

HEATH, R., DEMPSEY, C. W., FONTANA, C. J. *et al* (1980) Feedback loop between cerebellum and septal-hippocampal sites: its role in emotion and epilepsy. *Biological Psychiatry*, **15**, 541–556.

HO, M. (1984) Immunosuppressive effects during infections. *Birth Defects: Original Article Series*, **20**, 131–147. March of Dimes Birth Defects Foundation.

MARKOWITZ, P. I. (1983) Autism in a child with congenital cytomegalovirus infection. *Journal of Autism and Development Disorders*, **13**, 249–253.

MONEY, J., BOBROW, N. A. & CLARKE, F. C. (1971) Autism and autoimmune disease: a family study. *Journal of Autism and Childhood Schizophrenia*, **1**, 146–160.

OLDING, L. B., KINGSBURY, D. T. & OLDSTONE, M. B. A. (1976) Pathogenesis of cytomegalovirus infection, distribution of viral products, immune complexes, and autoimmunity during latent murine infection. *Journal of General Virology*, **33**, 267–280.

RAITEN, D. J. & MASSARO, T. (1986) Perspectives on the nutritional ecology of autistic children. *Journal of Autism and Developmental Disorders*, **16**, 133–143.

RITVO, E. R., FREEMAN, B. J., SCHEIBELL, A. B., DUONG, J., ROBINSON, H., GUTHRIE, D. & RITVO, A. (1986) Lower purkinje cell counts in the cerebella of four autistic subjects: initial findings of the UCLA–NSAC autopsy research report. *American Journal of Psychiatry*, **143**, 862–866.

SEVER, J. L., SOUTH, M. A. & SHAVER, K. A. (1985) Delayed manifestations of congenital rubella. *Review of Infectious Disease*, **7**, Suppl. 1, S164–S169.

STARR, S. E., TOLPIN, M. D,, FRIEDMAN, H. M., PAUCKER, K. & PLOTKIN, S. A. (1979) Impaired cellular immunity to cytomegalovirus in congenitally infected children and their mothers. *Journal of Infectious Disease*, **140**, 500–505.

STUBBS, E. G. (1976) Autistic children exhibit undetectable hemagglutination-inhibition antibody titers despite previous rubella vaccination. *Journal of Autism and Childhood Schizophrenia*, **6**, 269–274.

—— (1978) Autistic symptoms in a child with congenital cytomegalovirus infection. *Journal of Autism and Childhood Schizophrenia*, **8**, 37–43.

——, CRAWFORD, M. L., BURGER, D. R. & VANDENBARK, A. A. (1977) Depressed lymphocyte responsiveness in autistic children. *Journal of Autism and Childhood Schizophrenia*, **7**, 49–55.

——, ASH, E. & WILLIAMS, C. P. S. (1984) Autism and congenital cytomegalovirus. *Journal of Autism and Developmental Disorders*, **14**, 183–189.

SULLIVAN, R. C. (1975) Hunches on some biological factors in autism. *Journal of Autism and Childhood Schizophrenia*, **5**, 177–184.

TODD, R. D. & CIARANELLO, R. D. (1985) Demonstration of inter- and intraspecies differences in serotonin binding sites by antibodies from an autistic child. *Neurobiology*, **82**, 612–616.

WARREN, R. P., FOSTER, A., MARGARETTEN, N. C., PACE, N. C. & THAIN, W. S. (1985) Search for evidence that autoimmune mechanisms are involved in the development of autism. *Proceedings of the National Society for Autistic Citizens.*

——, ——, —— & —— (1986) Immune abnormalities in patients with autism. *Journal of Autism and Development Disorders*, **16**, 189–197.

——, —— & —— (1987) Reduced natural killer cell activity in autism. *Journal of Child and Adolescent Psychiatry*, **26**, 333–335.

WEIZMAN, A., WEIZMAN, R., SZEKELEY, G. A., WIJSENBEEK, H. & LIVINI, E. L. (1982) Abnormal immune response to brain tissue antigen in the syndrome of autism. *American Journal of Psychiatry*, **139**, 1462–1465.

10 Aspects of the evolutionary history of human social behaviour

LYNN WATERHOUSE

There are many disciplines which have been concerned with the study of human social behaviour, including anthropology, psychology, psychiatry, and sociology. Recently the rise of the discipline of sociobiology has involved a teleological reinterpretation of the purposes of human social behaviour. In sociobiology, acts of social behaviour are seen as having the goal of preservation of the individual, the individual's offspring, and the individual's family members. Darwin saw human emotions as having adaptive value in serving these goals, and present-day sociobiology extends Darwin's notions to consider the adaptive value of all elements of social behaviour.

Most sociobiological research and theorising has focused either on the adaptive value of specific acts such as food-sharing or anger, or on the value of domains of acts, such as altruism, aggression, or childcare. In this approach, sociobiologists have assumed that the domains of social behaviour they are defining have ethological validity. In fields other than sociobiology, researchers are not so sanguine about the functional analysis of units and domains of social behaviour. In the study of child development, for example, the presently defined domains of attachment and friendship are questioned as entities (i.e. are these developmental programmes or domains of social behaviour?). Moreover, the constituent elements which are theorised as components of these domains or entities are also questioned.

In most theorising, the larger question of what it means to be social is rarely addressed. In the present paper I would like to answer this larger question quite broadly, and state the claim that all social behaviour can be redefined simply as the co-regulation of the behaviours of two or more individuals. I would assert that the purpose of what we call 'social' behaviour is to enable us to conjointly regulate all sorts of activities. Co-regulation is adaptive in many circumstances because it confers the general benefit of support of one individual for another, and because more complex activities can be engaged in when individuals can act in concert.

We are not social simply to be social, nor are we social simply for the pleasure of it. 'Social' behaviour is pleasurable (when it is) because it is of critical importance for human beings to co-regulate a wide variety of behaviours for the adaptive success of the species. In sum, then, I am positing that all social behaviour serves to underwrite the process of co-regulation of other human activities.

Co-regulation of human behaviour exists whenever any individual does something to which another individual adjusts to, reacts to, or responds to. Co-regulation of behaviour is adaptive, it has helped all animals survive, and it depends on both innate propensities and learned skills in the behavioural repertoire of individuals.

In the discussion which follows, evidence from the evolutionary history of human social behaviour will be used to argue for the existence of three sets of mechanisms for the co-regulation of behaviour. These three sets of mechanisms will be considered in light of the pattern of child development, and some speculative notions concerning the relationship of these three sets of mechanisms to brain functions will be presented.

Evolutionary history

If social behaviour is co-regulation, and co-regulation mechanisms have arisen to help us survive, then whatever the crucial mechanisms of co-regulation are, it is likely that they arose at different times in human evolutionary history.

From a review of a variety of theories concerning the advent of human skills at different points in evolution, as well as a review of known regularities in modern human social behaviour, I have come to believe that there are at least three crucial and differentiable mechanisms of co-regulation, each of which has played a key role in the evolution of human social behaviour, and each of which operates in full force in current human social behaviour. These three sets of mechanisms are

    (a) the physical contact co-regulation of pair bonding

    (b) the face-to-face co-regulation of imitation and identification

    (c) the abstract memory-based co-regulation of symbol use.

In general function, these sets of mechanisms act in parallel: each set of systems provides the basis for the co-ordination of the behaviour of individuals. However, these sets of mechanisms differ in five ways. Firstly, it is likely that these mechanisms arose at different times in the course of human evolution. Secondly, the behavioural elements involved in each set of mechanisms are distinct. Thirdly, the specific goals which can be inferred for the sets of mechanisms are different. Fourthly, because it is likely that the sets of mechanisms arose at different times in human evolution, and because the behavioural elements of each set are distinct, it can be inferred that the underlying neurological functions which determine these sets of mechanisms may be different. Fifthly, the three systems operate at three different levels of requisite human contact: pair bonding requires physical contact: imitation and identification requires that individuals be in visual range of one another; and symbol co-regulation allows for the actual separation of individuals in time and space.

The plan of the present paper is to develop arguments for the three mechanisms theorised as distinct and to offer descriptions of these mechanisms which take into account developmental and neurological issues.

Pair bonding

In human beings there are two extended and specialised periods of pair bonding. The first is mother–infant pair bonding through the specific behaviours of nursing and caretaking, both of which involve contact between mother and child. The second period of pair bonding is male–female bonding through courtship and sexual behaviour.

While all mammals nurse their young, and while almost all animals have courtship and mating rituals, only primates have extended periods of care for their young, and only humans have extended male–female pair bonding. According to theorists (Lovejoy, 1981; Tanner, 1981), in the evolution of human social behaviour pair bonding was an adaptive development which arose subsequent to human bipedalism. With the freeing of the hands and arms, women could carry offspring, and men could carry food back to women and children. Women could also gather nuts, fruits, and roots, and share these provisions with their offspring and adult males.

Bipedalism dates back to at least 2 million BP (Campbell, 1985), and is most likely to have arisen as an adaptation to life on the African savannah. Hominids who could see above the grasses might have been more likely to see predators and thus survive.

The core of mother–infant pair bonding is the act of nursing. The core of male–female pair bonding is the sex act. In both cases the co-regulation of behaviour involves contact. In both cases the co-regulation determines aspects of the internal physiological functioning of both partners. Infants obtain food and reduction of physiological tension from nursing, while their mothers also obtain tension-reduction and receive the additional effect of curtailment of ovulation.

Sex partners too receive tension-reduction, and, like the nursing mothers, go through complex endocrine system changes as a result of the act.

Pair bonding in both cases is dependent on the co-regulation of behaviour which yields primary physiological rewards for both partners. This symbiotic relationship leads individuals to understand their partners as sources of pleasure. Infants have the primary reward of milk as food, and partners in both types of pair bonding experience the rewards of tension-reduction through tactile stimulation and warmth. Both forms of pair bonding involve olfactory recognition of the partners by one another. Not only do partners recognise one another by smell; it may be that the olfactory system entrains other functions. For example, it has recently been found that a female's smelling of male sweat can regulate that female's menstrual cycles (Monmaney, 1987).

From a series of studies of rat pup nursing, Hofer (1987) has concluded that the mother 'provides a combination of thermal, olfactory-alerting, and tactile stimulations that act together to exert a long-term control over infant behavioral responsiveness'. Hofer believes that in species with more complex cortical function than the rat (i.e. primates, humans), regulators may become increasingly more internalised. Hofer hypothesises that 'this might involve a shift from sensorimotor to higher-order associative and symbolic functions and from a dependence on interaction with the mother to a more flexible dependence on a variety of different social interactions'.

In pair bonding it is most likely that mother and child and male and female pairs experience the primary rewards of contact activities by means of the neural release of endogenous opiates. This internal reward/pleasure system ensures that there will be reproduction, and that offspring produced will be cared for successfully. In human beings, mother–child relationships are maintained until the death of child or mother, and many male–female pair bonds persist until the death of one of the partners. These lengthy associations we call love or attachment involve the co-regulation or co-ordination of behaviours over long periods of time. The generalisation of the mechanisms and behaviours of pair-bond co-regulation to other dyadic relationships over the course of human development may be the process which generates much of human affective social behaviour.

Stern (1984) has called the synchrony and reciprocity which is involved in mother–child interaction 'attunement'. He argues that this is crucial for the healthy development of the child. Freud wrote a great deal about the relationship between the tender feelings of identification love that exist between parent and child and the sensual feelings of object love that exist in sexual attraction. For Freud, a mature sexual relationship required that an individual overmaster the generalisation of identification love which arises initially in response to a desired sex object. For Freud both sensuality without tenderness and tenderness without sensuality were characteristic of most neuroses (Rieff, 1961). Thus for Freud the shift from mechanisms of parent–child co-regulation to mechanisms of male–female co-regulation carried the danger of an unresolved dualism.

Wilson (1983) has claimed that it is the relationship between the mother–infant pair bond and the male–female pair bond which creates human society. Wilson argues that 'although the two bonds are to be found in nonhuman species, they are found separately and not conjointly . . . it would seem that a conflict of interest between pair . . . bonds is possible in the human species alone'. It is the resolution of this conflict through the creation of the family unit and extended kinship relations that Wilson believes makes possible complex human society. Furthermore, just as Hofer has argued that the primary pair bond of mother and child generalises to all social behaviour, Wilson has argued that sexuality confers on human beings the individuation and self-consciousness which other species do not have.

The two forms of pair bonding, one which begins at birth, the other which begins at puberty, are associated in time of onset with two periods of neuronal change. Development of attachment generalisation in human infants corresponds closely to the corresponding period of synaptogenesis in the prefrontal cortex (beginning at eight months and reaching a peak at two years (Huttenlocher, 1979)). In summarising previous work, Goldman-Rakic (1987) has argued that this early period of excess synapse formation is associated with brain pruning, and that brain pruning begins again at adolescence and continues into young adulthood. Thus it is possible that the programmes of neural organisation which are argued to take place in infancy and adolescence are not only linked to the development of cognitive functions such as language and memory *per se*, but may also be associated with emergence of the complex unfolding of pair bonding and pair-bond generalisation.

Pair bonding is a complex form of co-regulation, the roots of which are ancient. The two forms (mother–infant; male–female) are likely to be the product of specialised neural functions, and both bonds involve multiple aspects of physiological co-regulation, as well as co-regulation of motor behaviours and affect. Generalisation from these elemental forms of co-regulation are likely to be the basis for much of human social behaviour.

Imitation and identification

By one million BP, people were living in small groups or bands on a recognition basis of 20–50 individuals. These groups had division of labour by sex, notions of kinship, exogamy marriage rules, and some established home sites (Campbell, 1985).

The mechanisms of co-regulation needed for maintaining small social groups are quite different from the mechanisms which serve to generate and maintain mother–infant and male–female pair bonds. The need for the development of social cohesion arises in the context of the existence of several groups living in the same region. Group definition is associated with group territory. Having a group territory means having access to all the food and water in that territory. In male-dominant primate societies, it also means having mating rights to and thus control of all the females in the region. It has been argued that the inter-group within-species competition that humans have engaged in throughout their evolutionary history has been exactly the mechanism for such rapid emergence of great intelligence (Alexander, 1979). Just as it is better to play tennis with a partner whose skills are slightly better than yours, close competition between subgroups of the same species may have been a powerful propellant for the evolution of human skills: more powerful than the inter-specific competition that most animals engage in.

When subgroups of the same species live close to one another in conditions where subgroup preservaticn is crucial because it means better control over resources, mechanisms which permit within-group co-regulation beyond the pair bond associations will become important. The set of mechanisms which aid within-group co-regulation appear to be (a) individual identification through face and body recognition, and (b) inter-individual mimicry.

The first mechanism — individual identification — enables group members to learn the fine details of faces and appearance so that group members can know if an individual is a member of their group or not. The second mechanism — mimicry — permits the refined co-regulation of both gross motor and fine motor behaviours, and permits the co-regulation of facial expressions and gestural and body posture displays.

The co-regulation of gross motor behaviours through imitation is adaptive in that it allows for the group or sets of members of the group to engage in behaviours simultaneously. This aspect of co-regulation occurs in many species other than primates. Usually a visual cue in the behaviour of an individual serves to trigger the same motor behaviour in the other group members. This enables the group to flee predators together, for example. However, co-regulation of fine motor behaviour means that joint tasks can be engaged in, thus permitting the development of more complex shared sequences of motor acts.

Unconscious mimicry of facial expression, gestural displays and body postures has been studied in detail in a variety of species, but relatively little has been done to study mimicry in human neonates (Field *et al*, 1982). The study of imitation and mimicry in adults has been limited almost entirely to the 'how to' realm of behavioural advice. It appears that such mimicry may provide an individual with some reassurance that the individual being faced may share the same affective state. Furthermore, it may actually be the case that imitation of affective expressions leads the imitator to experience some form of the emotion itself (Ekman *et al*, 1983). Moreover, patterns of affective display may be learned, and groups may set slightly different styles of affective display as part of group cultural evolution. Recently, Buck and Teng (as reported by Bower, 1987) have argued that their cross-cultural research findings suggest that the ability to interpret spontaneous non-verbal displays is innate but that the ability to produce such displays has both an innate and a learned component.

Kinship groups within the groups of 20–50 individuals would also mean that genetic predispositions to behave in certain ways might be shared across family members. This would mean that not only would the appearance of related individuals be somewhat more similar, their behaviours also might tend to be more similar. Thus sharing of affective states within kinships might make group cohesion easier at that sub-subgroup level.

Sharing similar behaviours and recognizing and knowing group members is crucial for a variety of group activities, including hunting, food-gathering, care of offspring, protection from predators, and competition with other subgroups for territory.

The co-regulation of behaviour based on identification and mimicry requires that individuals be within visual range of one another, but doesn't require physical contact, as does pair bonding. The co-regulation of behaviour through these mechanisms does not involve co-regulation of endogenous metabolic or endocrine functions for individuals, but may involve co-regulated sharing of (internal) affective states. Co-regulation processes of these mechanisms also permit that more than two individuals may share similar behaviours at the same time.

While many animals show mimicry of behaviours, such mimicry outside the realm of primates is strictly context-limited. Furthermore, the stimulus triggers to animal mimicry are usually small isolatable elements of behaviour or appearance. Unlike animal mimicry, human unconscious imitation appears to be multiply determined. A variety of aspects of a display may serve as triggers to imitation, and a variety of aspects of the display may or may not be imitated. It is important to note that unconscious motor and facial mimicry is not context-limited but functions rather as a constant of human social interactive behaviour. It is at once more pervasive and, in the event, more variable and more fleeting than the mimicry observed in other species.

Still more important to note is that 'monkey see, monkey do' is the basis for a vast range of human behavioural learning. Children and adults consciously and unconsciously copy the behaviours of others they observe in order to learn tasks that the others are engaging in. It is also true that children and adults copy the dress and mannerisms of those they know in order to be more like the others around them. Social institutions reinforce such behaviour with uniforms, behaviour codes, and the like. Teenagers may rebel against parents, but they will seek a group behavioural and appearance identity which requires an even stricter observance than the set of codes they are actively rejecting.

The neurological basis for face recognition is currently being explored in both humans and apes and monkeys. Prosopagnosia is a disorder involving inability to recognise faces, one's own clothing, categories of objects, and related sets of objects. Prosopagnosia results from right hemisphere lesions. Failure to imitate social behaviours is seen in a variety of psychiatric and organic disorders and has not been tied to or associated with any particular brain region. Damage to the frontal cortex, however, has been associated with the inability to stop imitating or performing a piece of behaviour once that behaviour has begun.

In developmental terms, complex imitation appears in its most florid form in toddlers and pubertal children. Toddlers walk around imitating adults, siblings and peers. They engage in parallel play, which is the side-by-side imitation of the play activities of one another. They can be observed imitating the facial expressions of adults in an exaggerated fashion. Teenagers imitate the behaviour of one another in small groups. This imitation may involve dress, mannerisms, body decoration, speech and other aspects of the presentation of self. Adults and young children too imitate others; however, the imitations are not so salient.

From identification springs the ability to create a constant group membership which all members can adhere to. From imitation springs the ability to work together and the ability to share experiences more exactly. These co-regulatory mechanisms permit the development of complex group sociability, and provide the basis for the origin of empathy: if I can identify you as an individual, and can imitate your affective expression, which in turn causes me to experience some version of your internal affective state, then I may 'know' how you feel. This, of course, in its turn may be the basis for empathetic responses.

Symbols as agents of co-regulation

The third set of mechanisms which arose for the co-regulation of human behaviour appeared on the scene very recently. Suddenly during the Upper Paleolithic, in the Mousterian period, there is evidence for art, ritual, play, care for the infirm, grave goods signalling care for the dead, music, and abstract symbols. These all appeared simultaneously at about 35 000 BP.

In an article refuting the evidence for complex culture in Neanderthals, Chase & Dibble (1987) have claimed that while Neanderthal people — who existed from roughly 400 000 BP to 40 000 BP — had material culture which required planning, gathering and tool-making, they nonetheless had a very simple and unimaginative culture. Chase & Dibble argue that although Neanderthals may have had affection for one another, as might be evidenced by burials of individuals who had clearly lived a good while past the event of severe injury, they did not have a symbol-based culture.

Current work on mitochondrial DNA has led to the intriguing hypothesis that modern humans (homo sapiens sapiens) have all descended from a single 'Eve' living in sub-saharan Africa two hundred thousand years ago. These modern humans took over from archaic homo sapiens. In a review of recent findings, Cann (1987) reports:

> "More than one hundred thousand years ago in Europe archaic humans (homo sapiens) gave rise to Homo sapiens neanderthalensis . . . Neanderthal people are thought not to have been ancestors of modern humans, because they themselves are not as old as the earliest Homo sapiens sapiens. And even if they were, it would be difficult to explain how they . . . overnight evolved into a new subspecies . . . the preponderance of paleontological evidence supports — though it does not prove — the theory that modern humans evolved in Africa and then emigrated to Europe and Asia, ultimately supplanting all their archaic cousins (who had previously emigrated from Africa as well)."

Taken together, findings and theory currently converge on the notion that the culture of modern humans should be dated after 40 000 BP. In Europe this makes the most likely candidate for the modern human line the Cro Magnon people. And what are the characteristics which allowed Cro Magnons to dominate and supplant Neanderthals so rapidly? Both groups had small-band organisation, both groups had tools and fire. Both groups had sufficient social organisation for planning hunts and planning burials.

Chase & Dibble argue that while Neanderthals may have had a size advantage which was considerable, what they lacked was symbol use. Neanderthals had tools, but no style in tool-making. Cro Magnon people had noticeable style in tool-making, and used elements of their environment to do a variety of things, all of which suggest an abstract understanding of symbols. Cro Magnon people adorned themselves with shells and bone bits. They collected flint flakes to make lithiphones (stone xylophones). They created pigment and used fire ash to draw pictures on cave walls. They also repeatedly painted a variety of abstract symbols thought to be associated with hunting and fertility rituals on cave walls. They outlined their own hands on cave walls. They created little figurines (Venus figures) of pregnant women. Most important, they had language with some form of syntactic structure. Instead of rough vocal displays, it is theorised that Cro Magnon people had noun and verb forms as well as a rudimentary system for ordering these forms.

They buried individuals with grave goods, and individuals found in such graves often had lived as cripples. This suggests that members of the group could lead a life after a major injury, which in turn allows the inference that individuals could live while directly dependent on help from the group.

I would like to claim that this phenomenal rise of symbolic culture meant that humans now had a new and quite remarkable ability. This new ability permitted humans to co-regulate their behaviour by something beyond physical contact and attachment, and by something beyond the direct recognition and imitation of the seen aspects of another's behaviour. The rise of symbolic culture meant that human social behaviour could be guided by abstractions. Whether we call these abstractions 'internalised symbols' or 'metarepresentations' (Chapter 3), such symbols function to control behaviour externally and directly: seeing the symbols on the cave wall or hearing another individual command your actions would constrain your behaviour. More importantly, such symbols also could serve to co-regulate the behaviours of individuals by internal and indirect means: from the stored image or stored statement (in human memory), an individual could co-regulate behaviour with others who were not nearby.

The ability to create words, images, marks, figures, symbols and signs which could provide a means for co-regulation across time and across space must have been an amazing source of power for these early people. And it still is an amazing ability. The sharing of behavioural patterns by means of observing and remembering symbols led to a complexity of social organisation beyond anything ever previously developed.

Social symbolism meant that ideas could be expressed and set in symbols in order that they might be used to guide behaviours in the group. Early people believed that their own created symbols would have power not only over human behaviours, but also over aspects of the natural world. Rituals were established which were designed to control presence of animals to hunt, growth of grains, and the patterns of weather.

Social symbolism also meant the development of abstractions which serve to more directly guide interactive behaviour. Language is the main tool of co-regulation. We express internal states, make claims about the world, and command the behaviour of others through language. We plan and agree to plans. We share hypotheses and co-ordinate memories. We regulate our perceptions of one another through interpretation and memory of the statements of one another.

Independent of language, there are a variety of abstractions which regulate interactive behaviour. Social psychologists have claimed that we begin all social interactions with an assumption of equality of status. That in itself is an abstraction about the structure of social hierarchies — we have to learn aspects of another's behaviours in order to understand the individual's 'group position'. Another critical abstraction is the idea that others have minds which can hold abstractions. This last is an extremely important manifestation of the abstracting ability.

Still another set of notions human beings have about one another is theorised by linguists as 'pragmatics' — social rules for the use of language in interaction. In sociolinguistics it is argued that human beings expect certain behaviours from those they interact with. These expectations are internalised assumptions or notions — that interaction participants actively wish to communicate, that they wish to tell the truth, that they wish to follow the culture's rules for interaction. Pragmatics also includes the set of rules which guide the productive expression of individuals — knowing when interruptions are allowed, knowing how to maintain a topic of conversation, and so forth. All of these abstract notions are thought to guide interaction in language. Internalised rules are only possible when abstractions can guide behaviour through memory.

Wilson (1983) has asserted that it is reasonable 'to propose that the emergence of language is contemporary with the discovery of other modes of signalling and symboling', even with the ritual skills of early human beings. Wilson believes that the performative character of rituals, however, means that they have a literalness and seeming utility which puts them at a pre-symbolic level. Wilson argues that something — an idea, a promise, a taboo — must be applied as part of a ritual for there to be representation of nature and content which turns ritual into a symbolising act.

Shamans are individuals who have been designated within cultures as conductors of ritual. According to Atkinson (1937), successful shamans are individuals on whose spiritual powers the group depends; however, shamans depend on the group to validate their work by acknowledging their shamanistic powers. In this circularity it is the imagination of all the individuals in the group working together, yoked by shared and unitarily conducted rituals, which generates the shaman's powers.

Shamanic power depends on the inherent promise of future events. Wilson (1983) has argued that promises are the cornerstone of human symbolising. For Wilson, a promise is a link between desire, purpose, means and ends, with an awareness of another's needs. Wilson further argues that promises are the precursors of teaching, 'for teaching is an activity that rests on forms without reality beyond themselves and prepares the learner without requiring him to experience the object taught'.

Conclusions

The mechanisms outlined here appear to have emerged at different times in the course of human evolution. Pair bonding emerged very early in hominid development after the development of bipedalism. Small-group co-regulatory mechanisms of imitation and recognition emerged by one million BP, and symbolising skills appeared quite recently, approximately 35 000 years ago.

All three sets of mechanisms come into play in the first year of life for modern humans. Infants experience the pair bonding of maternal closeness, and their relationship to family members involves a great deal of social mimicry (albeit primitive). A child's use of abstract symbols starts with the onset of speech at the end of the first year. In the second year a toddler may have a rapid development of language, as well as a rapid expansion of gestural displays. Toddlers begin parallel play. These emergent systems continue to develop and generalise throughout the life course. At puberty the additional richness and complexity of sexual behaviour unfolds. In all these mechanisms of co-regulation adaptive purposes are served as the individual depends on innate propensities and a great deal of learning to establish 'social behaviour'.

The present argument for three sets of mechanisms rests on the assumption that relevant behaviours have evolved. If these behaviours have been a part of human physical evolution, there must be some set of neurological functions which serves to trigger, shape, determine or maintain these various mechanisms. In some cases these underlying neurological functions can be hypothesised; in other cases they may not be able to be at present.

Pair bonding may involve the hypothalamus and the internal endogenous opiate system. Primary rewards must have associated internal 'rewards' generated by the nervous system. Deeper and older parts of the limbic system in general may also be involved in these processes.

Face recognition appears to be controlled by the right temporal cortex in human beings. Imitation processes may be a function of frontal and limbic systems.

Symbolic co-regulation by means of language depends on left temporal cortical function in most right-handed individuals. Other aspects of ritual, art, music, play and imagination most likely depend on a complex interplay of right and left temporal cortical function, as well as frontal cortical function.

Human social behaviour has often been thought to depend on human emotions, which in turn have been hypothesised to stem from the limbic system. Emotions are a shaky and slippery concept. A persistent question concerning emotions is whether they have reality as elements of neurological function, or whether they are mediators of motor reaction.

In the present model, the role of emotions is to serve co-regulation. There are a large number of theories about arousal systems and emotions. The most parsimonious interpretation in the light of current knowledge is that emotions are surface behaviour categories which have been reified by the culture. The actual internal functions are likely to simply be the arousal systems. One model of the arousal systems is that of Weil (1974). Weil postulates that emotions spring from three arousal systems — the somatic, the pleasure/unpleasure and the visceral arousal system. Weil associates differential states of these three arousal systems with distinct emotions as labelled in behaviour.

However emotions are understood or modelled and interpreted, in the mechanism outlined here emotions are seen as the effectors of states of change. Individuals co-regulate these basic states, as well as having these states as the basis for other aspects of co-regulation. Thus, emotions are both elements to be regulated in some situations, as well as being the 'grease' of co-regulation in other situations.

All aspects of co-regulation have some associated basis in neurological function, and all aspects of co-regulation are integrated in the developmental life-course of individuals. If one asks the question, 'What is the neurological basis for human social behaviour?', there can be no single answer. The answer must be that there are a variety of neurological bases for a variety of regulatory mechanisms, all of which we call 'social behaviour'.

Implications for autism

Brain development is a very active process. Most recent research suggests that neuron assemblies compete with one another for being the dominant connections. Efflorescence of synapses in early childhood gives way to brain pruning, and brain pruning increases at puberty into young adulthood. For all three mechanisms of co-regulation there is tremendous amount of learning which must take place. If neural assemblies form both through internal maturational processes and through learning, then anything which impairs normal neural maturation or limits learning in those neural functions which serve co-regulatory mechanisms will in turn serve to impair development of these crucial systems of co-regulation.

Becoming a social creature is a complex business and it has taken us a long time to become 'social' in the way that we are now. We know that autistic individuals have problems in the co-regulation of their behaviour with others. Our recognition of the range and variety of such problems may help us to better understand the nature of the spectrum of disorders aggregated under the heading 'autism'.

References

ALEXANDER, R. D. (1979) *Darwinism and Human Affairs*. Seattle: University of Washington Press.

ATKINSON, J. (1987) The effectiveness of shamans in an Indonesian ritual. *American Anthropologist*, **89**, 342–355.

BOWER, B. (1987) Faces of emotion: social or innate? *Science News*, **132**, 5 Sept., 150.

CAMPBELL, B. G. (1985) *Humankind Emerging*. Boston: Little Brown.

CANN, R. L. (1987) In search of Eve. *The Sciences*, Sept./Oct., 30–37.

CHASE, P. D. & DIBBLE, H. L. (1987) Middle paleolithic symbolism: a review of current evidence and interpretations. *Journal of Anthropological Archaeology*, **6**, 263–296.

EKMAN, P., LEVENSON, R. W. & FRIESEN, W. (1983) Automatic nervous system activity distinguishes among emotions. *Science*, **221**, 1208–1210.

FIELD, T. M., WOODSON, R., GREENBERG, R. & COHEN, D. (1982) Discrimination and imitation of facial expression in neonates. *Science*, **218**, 179–181.

GOLDMAN-RAKIC, P. (1987) Development of cortical circuitry and cognitive function. *Child Development*, **58**, 601–622.

HOFER, M. (1987) Early social relationships: a psychobiologist's view. *Child Development*, **58**, 633–647.

HUTTENLOCHER, P. R. (1979) Synaptic density in human frontal cortex — developmental changes and effects of aging. *Brain Research*, **163**, 195–205.

LOVEJOY, C. O. (1981) The origin of man. *Science*, **211**, 341–350.

MONMANEY, T. (1987) Are we led by the nose? *Discover*, **8**, 48–57.

REIFF, P. (1961) *Freud: the mind of the moralist*. Garden City, NY: Doubleday.

STERN, D. (1984) Affect attunement. In *Frontiers of Infant Psychiatry* (eds J. D. Case, E. Galenson & R. L. Tyson). New York: Basic Books. pp. 3–14.

TANNER, M. (1981) *On Becoming Human*. New York: Cambridge University Press.

WEIL, J. D. (1974) *A Neurophysiological Model of Emotional and Intentional Behavior*. Springfield, Ill: Charles Thomas.

WILSON, P. J. (1983) *Man the Promising Primate*. New Haven: Yale University Press.

Index